W9-AUM-653

Buried Alive!

Digging Out of a Management Dumpster

Also by the Authors

Confessions of an UnManager
Ten Steps to Jump Start Company Performance by Getting
Others to Accept Accountability

Buried Alive!

Digging Out of a Management Dumpster

by

Shane Yount, Anna Versteeg, Debra Boggan, John Pyecha with Linda Segall

THE OAKLEA PRESS

RICHMOND, VIRGINIA

First Edition

Buried Alive! Digging Out of a Management Dumpster © 2004 by Competitive Solutions, Inc. All rights reserved. Printed in the United States of America. No part of this book may be used or reproduced in any manner whatsoever without written permission except in the case of brief quotations embodied in critical articles and reviews. For information address The Oaklea Press, 6912 Three Chopt Road, Suite B, Richmond, Virginia 23226.

ISBN 1-892538-15-6

If your bookseller does not have this book in stock,
it can be ordered directly from the publisher.
Contact us for information about discounts
on quantity purchases.

The Oaklea Press
6912 Three Chopt Road, Suite B
Richmond, Virginia 23226

Voice: 1-800-295-4066
Facsimile: 1-804-281-5686
Email: Info@OakleaPress.com

This book can be purchased online at

http://www.LeanTransformation.com

Contents

Introduction

Take a few minutes to think about work:

• At the end of the day, have you crossed off all the items on your to-do list?

• Did the last "flavor-of-the-month" program accomplish the results it promised?

• Do the teams in your company and in your department really function the way they were designed to?

• Are your team meetings productive?

• Are your boss's meetings productive?

• Do you feel as though you are accomplishing anything worthwhile?

Be honest . . . if you answered "no" to any of these questions, you probably don't jump out of bed each morning looking forward to going to work. It's not that you don't *like* working. And it's not that you don't enjoy the people you work with. It's just that work has become, well, work. It's not fun anymore.

Work doesn't have to be *fun,* of course. But everyone — every worker — wants to believe he or she is contributing. And if you are a leader, you want to end the day feeling as though you have led the charge, your people have followed you and you have made headway in completing your mission.

But it's not always that way. Instead, what Competitive Solutions, Inc. has observed working with companies in a variety of industries, ranging from automotive manufacturers, to confectioners to petroleum providers, is that:

• They are struggling with how to create and sustain

an organization that operates with focus, urgency and accountability;

• Many leaders manage by personality instead of process;

• These leaders get the least out of their employees because they expect the least.

These leaders find themselves in a management dumpster filled with the trash of discarded and ineffective theories and programs. They are dumped on so often and so deeply by their bosses, their employees and their customers that they cannot climb out. They feel buried alive.

How in the world did leaders get to this state? It didn't happen overnight. Rather, it has been an evolutionary process. Typically, leaders go through a cycle:

• They *dictate.* They tell their employees what they want and how they want it done.

• When they find they cannot get the results they want, they *meditate* — by attending seminars, training and leadership development classes. They hope their "meditation" will give them the answers they desperately need to get the work done.

• After returning from training, they *hesitate* — because although they have learned and mastered isolated skills, they do not have a model in which to implement them in the real and immediate workplace.

• Because the leaders don't know how to put training into action, their situations *frustrate.*

• Frustration creates a strong urge to *annihilate,* because they can't get the job done as they know it should be done.

• Then, these leaders realize that if they want the job done, they have to do it themselve . They *demonstrate* what they want done to their employees. But by demonstrating, they *do*. And by *doing,* they become overburdened, sinking deeper and deeper into the mire of a management dumpster.

This is a sad state of affairs. But it can be fixed — and when it is fixed, leaders are able to climb out of their dumpster and — *facilitate!* That is, they design and deploy processes that give consistent focus, urgency and accountability.

The fix is simple: Instill three critical elements that are missing for effective leadership: *habit, discipline* and *structure.*

It's simple, but it's not necessarily easy.

Buried Alive! is the story about how one manager discovers that she is working in a management dumpster and how she — with the help of a colleague who has already dug himself out of his own dumpster — builds a foundation for process-based leadership and a ladder of non-negotiable steps to escape, never to return.

Buried Alive! is a blueprint for leadership that works because it outlines how leaders can create and sustain high-performance work systems.

If you know people who are working in a dumpster, use the blueprint to show them how to build the staircase to escape. And if, as you read the book, you discover you are in a dumpster, scrounge around, build your own staircase and climb out. You won't regret it.

And maybe you'll find that work will not seem quite as much like — well — work!

Chapter 1
Buried Alive!

Ima Manijer pulled her car up to her parking spot outside of her office in the Eniware Plant manufacturing compound. She shut off the motor and sat in silence for a few minutes, postponing as long as possible going in to work.

Ima was a manager at Eniware. Well, she *had* been a manager. Her title now — for the last couple of years — was group leader. That last reorganization ("re-engineering" "they" had said) was supposed to be "it." When "they" had reorganized into formal work groups, "they" promised that everyone would be able to "work smarter, not harder." So in "their" infinite wisdom, "they" had wiped out all of the supervisory jobs and reduced staff support in human resources, purchasing and accounting. They told everyone to hold meetings, solve problems and work together.

To Ima, it seemed like yet another rehash of quality circles, total quality management and self-directed work teams.

Ima didn't know if anyone was working smarter, but *she* knew *she* was working harder. With no supervisors to help her, it seemed that all of the details of the projects that her team came up with fell on her shoulders. And add to that recruiting, hiring and buying as well. "Yeah," Ima thought sarcastically. "We work together all right. The workers come up with all these great ideas and then I'm stuck with getting them done."

With that thought, Ima sighed and reluctantly

opened her car door to start her day.

Pulling her briefcase strap over her shoulder, she entered the building and shuffled along the long corridor toward her office, bent over like Atlas carrying the burden of the world on his shoulders. She felt that the load she was carrying was just as heavy. But the load was not in her briefcase; it was in her spirit.

As she inched down the hallway, she ticked off a mental to-do list in her mind: *"Gotta push production today; we're behind schedule. If we don't make it up, that customer will be on our backs. Darn that just-in-time manufacturing. And quality. Scrap was too high yesterday; so were rejects. It's gotta get better. Don't dare get any more complaints . . . huh, that's a pipe dream. Someone's always complaining. I have at least a dozen calls and letters to return to keep them off my back. If it's not the customers or the suppliers, it's the employees. Always wanting something.*

"And oh, yeah, performance appraisals. They're due today. Haven't even started on them. And can't forget the safety inspection. I was reprimanded on my appraisal last time because I let those inspections slide. And I have to remember the managers' meeting. Maybe I can find an excuse not to attend. What a waste of time! Hmmm … I have missed the last two. Better go. Maybe I can write up some of the appraisals and customer letters while the VP reads us her latest memo to employees and directives from management. I wonder if I can give appraisals to all 15 of my people this afternoon. Oh, darn! I almost forgot. I have a new employee starting this morning. Just what I needed. I don't have time to train him. Maybe he'll know how to run the machinery already . . . "

Each thought weighed Ima down even more. It was going to be a bear of a day.

At the same moment Ima had pulled into her parking space, Tim Leder — another manager-turned-group leader at Eniware — pulled into his space on the other side of the building. In contrast to Ima, who had sat behind the wheel for minutes after she turned off the key, Tim bounded from his vehicle. He couldn't wait to start the day.

Like Ima, Tim ticked off his to-do list as he trotted to his office. "Should be a good day," he mused. "First I'll meet with my team. We're on schedule and on target with our waste and reject targets. That's good news I want to share with them. Then I'll call the customer to let him know he can expect shipment on time. I have three performance reviews to hold today, but everybody's ready for them. And I'll end the day with a visit to my primary supplier. Yeah, should be a good day."

He was all energy and smiles.

Tim and Ima approached their building at the same time, but from opposite ends. Because Ima was so preoccupied with her thoughts, she didn't see Tim. But Tim caught sight of her as she came in the employee entrance. "Gosh," he muttered, "Ima doesn't look so good. I wonder if she's sick or something." He rushed down the hall to her.

"Ima! What's wrong?"

"Oh . . . hi, Tim. Wrong? Nothing's wrong." Ima glanced at him but didn't stop.

"Hey! Come on . . . what's up? You don't look so good." Tim walked alongside her.

Ima shook her head. "Nothing. Same old stuff. You know how it is. Just too much to do and not enough time to do it. And the morning hasn't even started yet."

"Really?" he asked. "Maybe I can help. What can I do for you?"

"You can't do anything. It's just the way it is. And it just keeps getting worse. Everyone wants something. I get pulled in every direction. Most days I don't know if I'm coming or going. And I can't seem to get anything done. The worst thing is that I don't feel like I'm doing anything worthwhile."

Tim listened compassionately as he accompanied Ima to her office. She unlocked the door and was about to say good-bye, when a big hulking fellow appeared from around the corner and confronted her. It was Monk E. Onurbak, one of Ima's more demanding employees.

"Hey, Ima," he shouted. "Wait up. I gotta talk to you." Monk wasn't known for wasting time on "niceties."

"What is it, Monk?" Ima asked impatiently. She didn't want to deal with him. In fact, she didn't want to deal with any of her "team" members. They always wanted something from her.

"It's my paycheck," said Monk. "You gotta do something about it. They shorted me four hours of overtime. I work, I wanna be paid. You owe me! Do something about it."

Ima sighed and took a memo pad out of her briefcase to make a note. "You couldn't wait until I got to my desk? You couldn't wait until I put my stuff away?" she whined to Monk. "Okay. Never mind. I'll fix it and get back to you."

Monk smirked, "Yeah, right. Later."

Tim watched Monk turn tail toward the break room and then looked back at Ima. He was shocked. Ima — already listless, stoop-shouldered and burdened with the weight of the world — was now virtually doubled over. He was genuinely concerned.

"Ima . . . here . . . let's go into your office and get you a glass of water. You look terrible!" Before she could protest, he pushed open the door, took her elbow and — without turning on the light — ushered her in.

Except that it wasn't *in*. It was *down*.

"Ima-a-a-a!" Tim yelled. His voice trailed off in a spiral as he plummeted to the "office" floor. He heard Ima land with a plop seconds before he reached the bottom. "Are you all right? Where are we?" He heard rustling, and a few seconds later, an overhead light snapped on. Ima stood knee-deep in a pile of papers with her hand on a light switch.

"What do you mean?" she answered, somewhat confused. "You know where we are. We're in my office. You opened the door yourself."

That's what Ima said, but that's not what Tim saw. He pushed himself up on his elbows and slowly looked around the room.

When he had stepped into Ima's "office," Tim had actually stepped out onto the ledge of a steep embankment. He had lost his balance, slid all the way down and landed on a pile of paper. Tim let his eyes wander around the room. "Your office? This is your office? Ima, I think you have a problem."

Ima sat down on a pile of manila folders. "Problem?"

she said sarcastically, tossing files up in the air. "I have a problem? Really? Yeah, I have a problem. My problem is that I can't get my work done."

Tim ignored her sarcasm. "Ima, do you sometimes feel like . . . uh . . . you are being dumped on."

"I would consider that an understatement. Why do you ask?"

"Take a look around you. What do you see? Take your time. Try to see what I see."

Ima sat there for a moment. She looked at the floor and saw papers piled deeper than she'd ever seen them before.

She looked at her desk — and couldn't find it. It was buried under manila folders and books.

She looked at the walls, and as she stared at them, they slowly lost their perpendicular perspective and began to slope steeply outward.

She looked at the ceiling, and instead of seeing fluorescent lights and dropped-ceiling panels, she saw a heavy-looking metal . . . lid.

"Where's the door, Ima?" Tim asked.

"Why, that's a dumb question! It's right over—" Ima pointed to the far wall. She jumped up and ran to the far wall, clawing at it. There was no door. She hurried to the adjacent wall. It was blank, too. She ran around the room, faster and faster, crying out: "Wait . . . what happened? Where is the door? What has happened to my office?"

Tim didn't answer. "What did happen to your office, Ima? What do you see?"

Ima stopped running in circles and stood in the middle of the room. Reality slowly hit her.

"Omigosh, Tim! Do you know what my office looks like?" The realization was hitting her. "It looks like a dumpster!"

"Yes, I noticed," Tim replied. He let his words sink in. "Ima, I have a confession to make. As soon as you turned on the light I could see the dumpster ... I could see it right away because — and you might not believe this —*I once worked in a dumpster, too.*"

Ima looked at him incredulously. "Impossible. I've seen your office. It's neat. Orderly. Everything has a place. And I see your reports each week. You're the star manager around here. Your department is leading in production and quality. You almost never have any customer complaints. *You* are the golden-haired group leader."

"No, it's true. I used to work in a dumpster," he replied. "I don't now, and I really enjoy my work today. But it wasn't too long ago that I was in a dumpster. It was so bad I dreaded coming to work. Just like you. I couldn't seem to get anything done. Every time I thought I was getting ahead, another disaster happened. Or management upped the ante. Or somebody quit and I had to get a new employee broken in. I was at the breaking point."

Ima listened as Tim shared his experiences as a dumped-on manager. He went on for some time, telling her one story after another of crisis management and barely averted disasters. With each confession he made, she first shook her head in disbelief and then she nodded in understanding.

"You're describing me!" she whispered.

Tim ignored her insight and continued telling his story. "It got so bad, Ima, that one day when I opened my office door, I slid down into the dumpster."

What is a management dumpster?

You know what a dumpster is. It's the commercial trash and garbage receptacle you find behind most businesses. Every night, the janitor empties discards from offices into this large bin, characterized by sloping sides that allow garbage to slide easily in, and a heavy steel top, which is weighted sufficiently to keep stuff from getting out.

Commercial dumpsters serve a valuable purpose: They provide a place to get rid of unwanted "stuff." The purpose is served admirably, as long as they are emptied regularly. But the purpose is defeated if the dumpsters are allowed to overflow. Then they become unsightly havens for vermin and health hazards to the environment.

A management dumpster is similar: It's an emotional and mental trash bin for managers. Management dumpsters accept workplace garbage — complaints, problems, discarded programs and whining — of employees, suppliers, customers and even bosses! As long as the dumpster is emptied regularly, it serves a purpose. It acts as a safe place for employees, vendors and bosses to vent.

Like its commercial counterpart, the management dumpster keeps a lid on all the different types of trash thrown into it. And just like the commercial dumpster, when the management dumpster is overflowing with garbage, it smells bad, looks worse and becomes a health hazard to the work environment.

"Just like we did a few minutes ago!" Ima interjected.

"I slid down, down. It was so bad, so very bad! When I reached the bottom, I could find no way out. *I was buried alive.*"

"What? I can't believe it!"

"I was so buried under everything everyone threw at me." Tim continued. "I sank so deep I couldn't climb out."

Ima's mouth fell open. She shuddered and looked around. "Tim, I think I'm buried. The door is gone. I don't see a way out. What am I going to do?"

Her words dripped with despair. Suddenly she brightened. "Wait a minute! You got out. You're here with me now. So you must know how to get out of here. Tell me. Please! How did you get out?"

"For a long time, I just wallowed in all of those management discards in my dumpster," Tim continued. "I couldn't find a way out. Or maybe I just wasn't ready. But one day, I got sick and tired of being sick and tired, and I decided I had to climb out. And the best part is — when I escaped, I realized that I would never have to be dumped on again."

He stopped talking. They sat quietly for what seemed like an eternity. Finally Ima whispered in a choking voice, "You know, despite everything — this dumpster — I really want to do a good job. It's just that no matter how hard I try or how many hours I work, I can't do it.

"It wasn't always like this. I remember a time when I looked forward to coming to work each day. It was fun. I liked helping my employees. I looked forward to helping solve my customers' problems. And I was really proud to make my goals … I don't know when or how it changed, but it did. But now I can't stand it any more . Please, please help me. Get us out of here. You know how to do it. Please share the secret. Please." She whispered her plea almost in tears, then got up and started clawing the sides of her dumpster.

Tim leaned back on a mound of memos. He could see that Ima was beginning to understand that the dumpster was more than just unfiled papers and disorganized memos. It was something much, much deeper and broader.

As he watched her whimper, he thought that maybe — just maybe — Ima had reached her bottom. Maybe — just maybe — she was ready to climb out of her dumpster.

"Ima, come and sit down. It's going to be all right. You're right; there is a way out. I learned how to do it and climbed out of my dumpster. And I'll tell you the secret."

Chapter 2
The Secret

Ima sagged to the floor in front of Tim. "What is it? What's the secret?"

Tim reached for the canvas backpack he used as a brief case. He pulled it toward him and rummaged for a few minutes. He finally pulled out a heavy-looking rectangular object wrapped in layers of protective burlap and tied with a yellow ribbon. He offered it to Ima.

"Ima, when I was buried in *my* dumpster, I found the secret. I've carried it around ever since, just so I won't forget it. It's right here. And I'm going to pass it on to you. *This* is the secret."

Ima took the rough-looking object. Its weight surprised her. She yanked on the ribbon and began to unwrap it. "This is the secret?" she asked, confused.

"That's it," said Tim.

Ima pealed the burlap aside and saw an oversized paving brick inscribed with one word in big capital letters:

NON-
NEGOTIABLES

"I don't understand. How can non-negotiables be the secret?" Ima asked.

"It *is* the secret," said Tim. "Non-negotiables. It's the

cornerstone. If you can accept the concept that some things are 100% non-negotiable, we can build a foundation and steps, and climb out of this dumpster."

Ima sat down and stared at the brick for several minutes. She carefully fingered each letter of the word, one at a time, outlining them to commit them to memory. She hefted the brick. It was heavy. Solid. It felt as if it could withstand any load.

She shook her head — not in rejection, but in confusion. "I really don't understand. Everything we've been told for . . . so many years. We've been taught to be 'nice guys.' They've told us we have to listen. We shouldn't demand. We have to 'get the consensus of the group.' To me, that's negotiation, at least a kind of negotiation, since doing those things certainly wasn't what I wanted to do and there was a lot of giving in.

"In fact, I remember when I was made a manager. Gosh, it's been almost 20 years. When I wanted something done, I just told my employees to do it!"

Tim allowed himself a small, almost imperceptible smile. He remembered those days, too. He could smile now, but back then, he knew that he had been known as the "dictator." All managers had been. They ruled with an iron fist: "Do it my way or find the highway." It had worked — to a point.

But the problem with dictatorship was that too many employees did only what they were told. When they finished a task, they just sat there, waiting for an order to do something else. And if there wasn't anything else to do, they got paid for doing nothing. Paying people premium wages to sit around and do nothing was the downfall of American industry.

He recalled taking a tour of an automotive-parts manufacturing plant during his early days in management. As he and his tour guide walked through the press room where huge presses turned sections of sheet metal into exhaust-system parts, he saw workers sitting around idle, smoking and drinking soda.

"Why are those guys just sitting there?" he had asked the guide.

"They're either waiting for maintenance to come and fix something or they've finished their work already," the guide replied. Then he added derisively, "A lot of the guys have figured out how to get eight hours of work done in six."

Not a good use of time, minds or muscle, Tim had thought. But that was back in the days when employees only did what they were told to do, and working smarter meant figuring out a way to sit around and get paid for doing nothing.

Dictatorship didn't really inspire loyalty or dedication.

Tim snapped out of his reverie and turned his attention back to Ima.

She resumed thinking out loud. "Telling people what to do seemed to work all right. I guess it wasn't a perfect way to manage, but it seemed to work back then. But the bad times came and what we did wasn't good enough. Unlike other 'bad times,' this time quality fell along with productivity and customers were demanding quality. That had never been a real problem in the past, but now a lot of foreign competition had sprung up. These foreign companies were able to produce cheap but good.

"So they decided we had to learn new ways to manage and they sent us to training. 'Learn to be a leader,' they said. We learned all this management and leadership *stuff*, all right. Some *stuff*! Seems that every time I went to school I came back with more work and only theoretical tools to do it. Nobody backs you up! I get so mad sometimes. It's so *frustrating!*"

Ima rambled on, mumbling to herself mostly. Tim could see her aggravation and anger mount. He understood. He had been there.

"In theory it all sounded so good," Ima went on. "Getting employees to take on more responsibility so that you didn't have to stand over them every minute. They told us, 'Empower your employees! Listen to them.' To me, that's negotiation, because when I listen to my employees and do what they want, I don't get to do what I want. I give in.

"Now you're telling me not to negotiate? That *non-negotiables* are going to get me out of this dumpster? I just don't see how."

"Uh, huh," Tim nodded. Ima took a breath and went on.

"I don't know, Tim. Asking me not to negotiate is just so *different* from everything they've preached at us. It's gotten to the point that my employees expect me to negotiate! They don't want me to dictate to them! It'll never work."

"Before you immediately reject the idea, Ima, think about it for a while. Think about the last meeting you held with your employees."

Ima sat quietly for a few minutes, contemplating

"non-negotiating" with her employees. She unconsciously rubbed the brick as she recalled a recent departmental meeting.

Her group had been grappling with a quality problem identified by a customer complaint. (Actually, Ima parenthetically admitted to herself, they were pretty good at problem solving. Maybe all that training *hadn't* been wasted.) During that meeting, the team had had a lively discussion that ended in a decision to gather more data. Collecting the information would require each person to take on one extra task each day. Everyone in the group agreed that the extra work would be worth it. Everyone, except Monk.

"Now look," Monk had shouted, "I won't do it. It's not in my job description." Monk didn't discuss things; he refuted them.

The group grew silent while Monk carried on. No one looked him in the eye. No one said a word. Monk ranted. "There's no way that information is going to help anyway, so there's no point in making us do this. Besides, I know I can't get all my regular work done *plus* get those samples. I know there's no overtime for this. Can't be done. Forget it."

Once Monk stopped ranting, the room went completely silent. Finally Ima said, "Well, let's think about this and see if we can come up with another solution at our next meeting."

Tim broke into Ima's thoughts. "What happened in the meeting, Ima? Did it go like it should have?"

Ima shook her head. "No. We had all agreed on a course of action, then Monk decided he didn't want to do the extra work. So we didn't act on the solution."

Tim nodded. "That used to happen to me all the time. That's not negotiation. And it's definitely not managing by consensus. That's giving in. It's managing by personality — in this case, Monk's personality — *not* by business processes."

Ima pursed her lips and nodded. "I let Monk override the decision of the group. So what you're saying is that if I had *non-negotiated* that meeting — *hadn't* allowed Monk to intimidate us — we would have fixed the quality problem."

Tim nodded and let her process her thoughts.

Finally she said, "Even if non-negotiating only applied to Monk, my life would be a lot easier. Tim, I'm ready," she whispered. *"I promise to non-negotiate anything you tell me to."*

What Are Non-Negotiables?

Non-negotiables are minimum processes that all leaders and teams perform to remain consistent, focused and accountable. An organization's senior-most leadership team defines non-negotiables for key areas, including communication, accountability, business scorecards and behavioral systems.

A process is a set of visible and auditable activities and behaviors that are performed consistently to produce expected outcomes. When leaders address key areas (communication, accountability, business scorecards and behavioral systems) with a process-based mindset, outcomes for each area become predictable — because all organizational employees work within clearly defined and commonly understood parameters.

Non-negotiables establish minimum standards for performance and behavior. They form the cornerstone of process-based leadership. Non-negotiables give leaders a framework to give their organizations habit, discipline and structure, which in turn create and sustain a sense of urgency, a clear and concise business focus, and drive a sense of collective accountability.

Chapter 3
The Foundation

"I'm ready, Tim. This isn't how I want to live my work life. I hate it! Just tell me what we have to do to get out of here," Ima said.

"The non-negotiables brick is the cornerstone, Ima," Time said. "We've got to set it in place to make the base of our staircase. But this one brick is not enough. It's strong. It'll carry a lot of weight. But we need a broader base on which to build our steps. And you can see that we need several steps to climb out of here." He looked upward. The wall they had to scale rose high.

"What I learned when I was buried in my dumpster is that everything we need to climb out is already here," Tim continued. "We have to scavenge and find it. It's all here. It just hasn't been put together right."

The floor of the dumpster was littered with the discards of the Eniware Plant's various management programs that had been tried and tossed away over the years. Tim and Ima began to sort through the trash.

"What exactly are we looking for, Tim?"

Tim chose not to answer her directly. He knew that discovery was a better teacher. "You'll recognize it when you see it, Ima."

Ima began separating and tossing. She found pieces from the different programs Eniware had tried over the years. She had gone through all of the training programs and as a manager had implemented each one. Invariably, after six months to a couple of years, each of these programs — which had promised to fix the plant — had faded away and was replaced with yet another one. As the frequency of programs accelerated, so had the skepticism — of managers and of employees.

As she examined the components of each program, Ima became intrigued and started stacking them up. "You know, Tim, some of these ideas weren't too bad. They just got out of hand." The stack included things like *delegation management, quality circles, teamwork, empowerment, total quality management* (also known as TQM), *re-engineering* and *self-directed work teams.*

"Why do you think they didn't work?" he asked.

She sat back on her haunches and looked off into space to gather her thoughts. "I'm not sure. I think the ideas behind a lot of these programs were okay. Maybe more than okay. Like delegation, probably the first attempt to get work done more efficiently. Delegate, they had said. Only problem, when most of us delegated, we told our employees exactly what to do and how to do it instead of just telling them the outcome we wanted and letting them have a go at it. It took so long to delegate, a lot of us ended up doing it ourselves. It was easier.

"*Teams* was another program that seemed pretty good, too. Employees working together to solve problems and run their work. On paper, it looked like the company could save a lot of money by getting the employees to do the work of a layer of management. We could save a lot of money by eliminating a layer of bureaucracy. But when the teams were left on their own, they lost focus of the bigger picture. And the work that supervisors used to do, well, managers got stuck with it. You don't suppose . . . " She was struck by an insight and her voice trailed off as she frantically dug into the refuse again.

"Tim! Look! I think I've found it. One of the building blocks. Look!"

Tim waded through the paper and looked at the brick Ima had found in the debris. It was inscribed:

BUSINESS FOCUS

Ima's excitement mounted. "I think a lot of those flavor-of-the-month programs failed because they lost sight of their business focus! It's kind of like a story I once heard:

"Every day this worker would go out at 7 a.m. and turn a valve on and return at 3 p.m. and turn it off. It took him at least 30 minutes, going and coming from his other work station. He did this for 22 years, faithfully.

"Finally, it was time for him to retire. A young worker was hired to replace him and his boss asked the older worker to show the newcomer the ropes. So the new guy followed the older worker around the next day. At 7 a.m. they walked out to the valve. 'Every morning you turn this valve on,' the experienced worker instructed, 'and every afternoon, you come out and turn it off at 3 p.m.'

"'What does the valve control?' asked the new worker. 'Beats me,' answered the older fella.

"But the question bothered him. And on his last day at work, he asked his boss. 'Just what does that valve do that I've been turning on and off every day for the last 22 years?'

"Startled, the boss answered him. 'You're still turning that valve on and off? That pipe hasn't done anything for the last 15 years. It isn't connected to anything.'

"The worker had been so caught up in doing his job and only his job that he never saw the big picture or questioned how his work contributed to the company's goals. He didn't have a business focus.

"I think," concluded Ima, "that some of these programs failed because the teams and the employees never looked beyond what they were doing for themselves. They never focused on the business. They just focused on their jobs. And I suspect others failed because of that personality thing we were talking about earlier. As managers, we managed by personality and gave in instead of standing firm and focusing on the long-term business goals. Standing firm. Why, that's non-negotiable!"

Tim smiled broadly. He helped Ima plant the brick adjacent to the keystone.

She looked at the two bricks. "Yeah. Non-negotiables and business focus. That focus, I think, has to be very clear and pointed. You know, so that it can't be easily lost."

Tim nodded and patted the bricks. "We've got a good start on this foundation, but it's not stout enough yet. We need a couple more bricks to make sure it's broad enough to hold the stairs we need to build to get out of here. Let's get back to work."

They both returned to their piles of folders and papers and dug in again. Tim attacked his pile with the same appetite that he brought to his work. He worked fast and efficiently, handling each piece of paper only

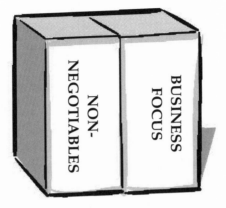

once. Neither manager talked for a long time. After about a half hour, Tim looked up to see how Ima was doing. He frowned at what he saw.

She was curled up comfortably in a nest that she had made out of old memos. She would casually reach for a folder, open it slowly and read each piece of paper thoroughly, savoring the history and memories that it brought back. In the last 30 minutes Tim had created a discard pile three feet tall. Ima's was barely a quarter of that.

"Ima!" Tim barked. "What are you doing?"

"Huh? I'm going through these papers, just like you."

"I don't think so." Tim pondered how to make his point. "Do you want to get out of here?"

"Yes. Of course."

She didn't get it, he thought. "If you want to get out of here, how come you aren't working hard at finding those remaining foundation blocks? How come your pile

What is a clear and concise business focus?

To understand the concept of a clear and concise business focus, you must first understand "process."

A process is a set of visible and auditable activities and behaviors that are consistently done to produce an expected outcome.

A clear and concise business focus keeps all leaders and teams consistently on target to achieve the mission and goals of the organization.

This business focus is achieved when all employees understand how their performance affects the top five to ten business metrics of the organization, as well as how these top metrics affect overall organizational performance.

of discards isn't as big as mine?"

Ima blushed at the reprimand. She stammered an excuse: "Well, uh, I'm working at it. Uh . . . " She was at a loss for words, because she knew that she was in the wrong. "I'm sorry, Tim. You're right. I *do* want to get out of here, and I need to do my share. The truth is ... and I'm embarrassed to admit it ... I got comfortable with the *doing* and lost sight of why we were doing it ... I lost my business focus ... And when that happened, I got comfortable working at my pace instead of what was needed to get the job done. *I'm guilty of doing what my employees do."*

She paused and smacked the palm of her hand against her forehead. "My gosh, Tim. Do you suppose ..." She quickly burrowed into the pile in front of her and exclaimed. "Look, Tim! I think I've found the last two bricks that we need! Quick, look!"

She scraped the papers aside and there they were — two bricks, each with one word written on them.

URGENCY
ACCOUNTABILITY

"I think these are the remaining bricks that we need for our foundation," she said. "It's what has been missing from *all* of those programs. A sense of urgency. And accountability. I know that my employees do their work without *a sense of urgency*. They kind of think that work is like a country club. It's like . . . if we get it done, fine. But if we don't, well, there's always tomorrow. What they don't realize is that there may not be a tomorrow if they don't get off their behinds!

"And *accountability*. They haven't accepted their part in making success happen. It's like when Monk threw a monkey wrench into our last meeting when he refused to take on that extra task. It was part of his job — whether or not it was in the job description. It was his job — *everyone's jobs* — to make a quality product and we had it within us to do it. But we didn't take responsibility for it ...

"Tim, I really understand now why establishing non-negotiables is the cornerstone. It's a thread that runs through every other process. Am I right, Tim? Am I?" she asked eagerly.

"Ima, I knew you could find the paving bricks to build a strong foundation. Let's get these laid so that we can start building the stairs."

Tim picked up one of the bricks, Ima the other. They planted them next to the two they already had placed. The foundation was now ready.

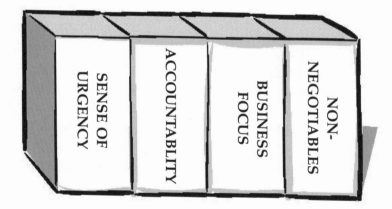

Chapter 4
Home Team!

Tim and Ima finished laying the four foundation bricks and cleared away an area around them. They eyed their handiwork with pride.

"That's a good start," said Tim. "Now for the hard part — building the steps. He eyed the top of the dumpster. It was a long way up.

"How many steps do you think we're going to need?" Ima asked. She could barely make out the rim of the heavy lid.

"Well, I'm not really sure yet. It's going to take several. It's a looong way up! Let's get going. You start in that corner. I'll start in this one. Remember — stay focused, work quickly, do your job and don't compromise." Tim smiled as he paraphrased the premise of the staircase's foundation. He wondered if Ima "got" it.

They slogged to their respective spots, rolled up their sleeves and dropped to the floor to begin a systematic search for the building materials. Each worked diligently and quickly. The papers flew and the piles grew. Minutes ticked away.

"Ima! I think I've found what we need for the first step!" Tim excitedly gathered up the material and ran to the base they had built. "Here! Look!" He dumped his pile next to the bricks.

Ima rushed over. She could barely contain herself. Maybe they could quickly and easily build these steps and get out of here. She didn't want to be buried alive.

But when she saw what Tim had dumped on the floor, her face fell.

"Tim, this can't be the stuff we need for the first step. It's just—" She looked down at the pile. On assorted individual papers two words were spelled out: TEAM MEETINGS.

"What's the matter, Ima? I thought you'd be happy that we can begin building our steps."

"Tim, it's just that team meetings can't *possibly* be one of the steps. We've had meetings — even *team* meetings — for years. They just don't work. They're a waste of time."

Tim considered Ima's comments. "Earlier you were telling me about a recent departmental meeting you held. If I recall, you said everyone had agreed to a solution to a quality problem. Everyone except Monk."

"Yeah, that meeting was a catastrophe," Ima said. She had given in to Monk. That was *managing by personality,* she now realized. But Monk's intimidation had happened at the end of the meeting. Unfortunately, the meeting had gone badly from the time it had been scheduled to begin — 9 a.m. sharp.

She had been there at 9 a.m. So were a few other employees.

At 9:18 the meeting was still short three people.

Ima looked around the group and took a mental roster. "Where are Monk, Susan and Tom?" she asked the other group members.

Stanley mumbled without looking up from the crossword puzzle he was working on. "I think they're still in the break room finishing their coffee and bagel. They were having a pretty good time."

Ima decided to begin without them. "All right. We'd better get started." They began to discuss the quality problem their customer had complained about.

At 9:25, Monk and Susan pulled open the door and loudly burst into the meeting. "Hey, dude! What did we miss? Probably nothing," Monk guffawed.

"Actually, Monk, you missed quite a bit. Janice, why don't you fill them in on what we were talking about?"

Janice, the group recorder, scanned her notes and started reading from them. The group spent several more minutes recapping their previous discussion. In the middle of it, Moe began arguing with Janice.

"Hey, I didn't say that our customer's specifications were too tight. I just said that when the tolerance was that close, it was almost impossible to take a good read. That's a big difference," Moe bickered.

"No, you didn't," said Janice. "I'm taking the notes. I know what I heard."

The squabble went on for several more minutes, with

other employees piping up. Ima finally refereed in disgust: "It doesn't make any difference. Let's just get on with it!"

Once that argument was settled, the discussion had gone smoothly, she had thought at the time. But as she sat in the dumpster and replayed it in her mind, she realized that it had been dominated by only Moe, Janice and Monk.

Stanley had never said one word during the meeting. In fact, she remembered, he had kept his nose in his crossword puzzle the whole time. He probably hadn't even been aware of what was being discussed.

For half of the meeting, Jennifer and Monique had whispered and giggled like two school girls. It was a sure bet they hadn't been snickering about the quality problem.

And for 20 minutes of the meeting, the entire group had complained about management's latest memo about an upcoming training program — a topic that wasn't even on the agenda.

When the meeting had finally ended and everyone went back to work — or the break room — Ima realized that Tom had been a complete no-show. She wondered where he had been for that hour.

No, she thought as she sat in her dumpster looking at the papers that spelled out "team meetings," it hadn't been a good meeting. But even worse, it was typical of all her departmental meetings.

"I can see you are thinking about that meeting, Ima. Now tell me, did the meeting start on time?"

"No."

"Did all of the employees attend — and participate?"

"No." She shook her head.

"Did the discussion stay on topic?"

She shook her head again.

"And did you discipline those employees who came in late or didn't show up?"

"What? Discipline them? Like, *punish* them?" Ima had never heard of anyone getting punished for not coming to a meeting.

"Yeah. Did you hold them *accountable* for their behavior?"

"Well, no." Suddenly the light bulb went off. "My gosh! How could I be so dumb! Here we are, literally sitting on the building blocks, and I can't even see them! Those team meetings didn't work because (a) they weren't focused on business issues, (b) there was no sense of urgency, (c) my employees didn't accept any responsibility for their actions, and — *most important* — (d) I hadn't insisted that participating on the team was *non-negotiable.*" Ima let all of that out in one breath. She inhaled and looked at Tim for guidance.

"By George, I think you've got it!" Tim responded.

Ima's elation lasted only for a few minutes. She shook her head again. "Yes, I see why my departmental meetings have failed. But I have to admit that some of the project teams I've been on were actually pretty good. We really worked well together. Everyone participated and we got the projects done."

"What was the difference between those teams and your departmental meetings?" Tim asked.

"Let me think. I believe it was that the people on

those project teams actually volunteered. Or they were handpicked to be on them because of their skills and willingness to work on extra things. So they wanted to do a good job."

Tim nodded. He knew that hand-picking also manifested managing by personality: Leaders picked employees they could count on and allowed non-participating or negative employees get away with not participating. But he decided to let Ima figure that one out. He asked, "Uh huh. And once the projects were completed and rolled out, did everyone else accept their roles in making the solutions happen?"

Ima thought about a team she had been invited to participate on, along with several other managers. Morale had been bad — real bad. You could see it in the demeanor of the employees. Work was not a happy place.

Worse, poor attitude was affecting quality and productivity: Absenteeism was at an all-time high, along with employee turnover, which hovered at almost 50% during one six-month period. And workers' comp costs skyrocketed.

Someone in top management decided that the reason for the morale problem was because managers did not recognize the good work of their employees.

The vice president hand-picked a group of managers who had aspirations of career advancement and assigned a directive: Come up with a good old-fashioned employee recognition program.

The managers were excited at the prospect of curing a major organizational problem. They met for three hours a week for six weeks and finally emerged with what they called a "pat on the back" program.

It worked this way: Each week, every unit manager was to select one employee in his department who had done good work that week. The manager would give the employee a sticker and a certificate that said "a pat on the back." Their names would appear in the company newsletter.

They presented the program to the vice president. She loved it. She was sure it would cure the morale problem. So she gathered all of the unit managers together and gave them a directive:

"Starting this week, I expect each of you to pat an employee on the back."

The managers — all of them except those who had designed the program — hated the program. If anyone had asked them — and no one had — they would have pointed out the flaws in the program design: that few employees, in their opinion, did more than marginal work and therefore didn't deserve recognition. And that employees would easily see how contrived the program was and would laugh at management behind their backs.

The first week of the program, all of the managers reluctantly gave pats on the back. The second week, fewer did. And by the third week, only those managers on the committee recognized their employees.

And the vice president never followed up to make the managers accountable for the program. By the end of only the second month, the program died a silent death.

Ima snapped out of her reverie. "No. Even though

the team worked together, no one else shared in the responsibility for the project, because they weren't part of it from the get-go. I think, maybe—" She struggled to find the reason why this type of team had failed. "Maybe . . . by handpicking the committee members to select those who obviously were hard workers, it was managing by personality?" She wasn't quite sure. Almost, but not quite.

Tim raised his eyebrows and nodded.

She continued to process the reasons why the team had not succeeded. "And the managers who had not been part of the team were not held accountable, and the VP hadn't made that accountability non-negotiable! In fact, the VP didn't even hold herself accountable!" She beamed at her insight. "Now I do think I've got it!" she laughed.

"That's right," Tim responded. "*All* of those four bricks have to be in place. They are processes, not events. And if team meetings are not held with all of them in place, the efforts of the team or group are doomed to fail."

"Maybe this." She pointed to the pile with "team meetings" written all over it. "This is the stuff the first step is made of." She began rummaging to get the papers in order.

"What's this?" Ima asked. She pulled out some waste paper that had words written on them. She placed the pages on the floor in no particular order, much like an anagram. They read:

IS NOT OPTIONAL
HOME TEAM
EVERY MEMBER
OF THE ORGANIZATION
IS ON A
MEMBERSHIP

"I don't think you have them in the right order. Let's try moving them around," said Tim.

They worked fervently together, working the papers like a puzzle. Finally, they came up with two sentences:

EVERY MEMBER OF THE ORGANIZATION IS ON A HOME TEAM. MEMBERSHIP IS NOT OPTIONAL.

"You know, Tim, I think this actually makes sense! If everyone in the company — including the head honchos, who generally think that teamwork is for everyone else except them — were on a home team and if that were a non-negotiable item, then the whole business organization would have a consistent look and feel and structure. I mean, having a rule like this is pretty basic. It would eliminate a lot of those problems we've had with teams before. It's so basic, it's like . . . *the first step!*"

With that, Ima sat back on her haunches and grinned. She and Tim then used the materials and built a solid first step.

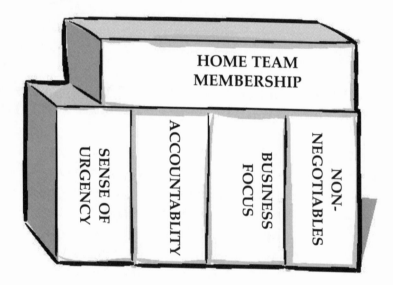

Every member of the organization is on a home team. Membership is not optional.

The first non-negotiable item in process-based leadership is membership on a home team. Everybody in the organization (regardless of his or her level or function) is on a home team.

A home team is defined as the natural work group — the boss and his or her direct reports. In a traditionally structured organization, a home team may be called a unit, a cell or a department. Natural work groups function well as home teams, because they are structured to focus on their contributions to the business. They are also configured to facilitate organizational communication.

Within an organization, any number of home teams exist, starting with the primary team — headed by the top leader in the business and his or her direct reports. The home-team structure then cascades throughout all organizational levels and functions. Team leaders are also team members. They lead teams consisting of their direct reports. And they participate on home teams that are led by their bosses and whose members are peers.

Belonging to a home team does not preclude participating on other types of teams, such as project teams. But because everyone is on a home team and because the home team operates with a clear and concise business focus, a sense of urgency and collective accountability, process-based leadership works.

Chapter 5
Communicate!

Finishing the foundation and first step energized Tim and Ima to finish their work. Ima was now driven with a sense of purpose and urgency. No more dawdling for her. She had learned her lesson, and her pile of discarded trash grew rapidly as she searched for more material to build the remaining steps.

Tim watched Ima's progress. She actually appeared to be content as she attacked her pile. He saw a broad smile slowly spread across her face.

"Hey, what's making you so happy?"

"This is great!" she responded excitedly, pointing to the stuff around her. "I really believe I've found the stuff for our next step."

Tim got up and went over to her. He looked over her shoulder at the stuff spread out in front of her.

"Is that what you're so happy about?" Spread about her were:

TWO LARGE PLASTIC BANNERS
AN ASSORTMENT OF MEMOS
E-MAIL
ELECTRONIC MESSAGING BOARDS
A BULLETIN BOARD
NEWSLETTERS

"Yeah, isn't it great! It's communication! And we're really good at it, so we have plenty of building materials!" She practically gloated over her find.

Tim examined each of the items closely without comment. He found:

- **Two large plastic banners painted in primary colors. One read:**

Safety begins with you!

The other said:

Great customer service begins with a smile!

- **A stack of office memos.** The top one read:

To: All employees
From: The vice president
Subject: Quality control
We have recently had a rash of returned out-of-specification product. From now on, use the Six Sigma quality method to maintain adherence to standards. Defects will not be tolerated.

Another read:

"To: All managers
From: The vice president
Subject: Performance appraisals
This memo is in regard to performance appraisals. All appraisals on your employees must be in my in box by 5 p.m. tomorrow. Make sure they are signed and dated.

Your own appraisals will be scheduled for next week. Fill out the appraisal form and give it to me by Monday morning.

The gist of the remaining memos was the same.

• **E-mails.** Lots and lots of e-mails. Some were simple letters between two individuals, straightforward exchanges of information or data.

Some of them, however, were virtual dialogues between two, three — even a dozen — people. To make sense of these e-mails, you had to go to the bottom and read upward.

Some of the e-mails came from across the country and around the world. A lot of them, however, were sent between people who sat about three feet apart.

• **An electronic sign** — the kind that scrolled and blinked its messages and tried to capture attention with cute little graphics, like cars driving along the bottom. This sign's lights still shined. It said:

Town hall meeting Wednesday at start of shift . . .

Take aim and go for the goal! United Way drive ends Friday. Have you given your Fair Share?

Good work Dept. 5 . . . 980 hours without a lost-time accident . . .

• **A bulletin board.** All kinds of things were thumb-tacked to it:

*Congratulations to Jim Smith for setting this month's
individual production record.*

*The number of customer complaints this
month is down.*

*The company picnic will be held on June 15 at the City Park.
We hope everyone will attend.*

A faded newspaper item reporting on the company's
record-breaking quarter.

A four-color magazine article complete with pictures
praising the innovative ideas generating from the plant
manager.

- **A bunch of newsletters.** There were:

  Companywide newsletters.
  Plantwide newsletters.
  Departmental newsletters.
  Customer newsletters.
  Quality newsletters.
  Training newsletters.
  And newsletters about newsletters.

He picked up each item, turned it over and around,
looked at it carefully from every angle, and put it down
— all without saying anything. The silence was almost
deafening. Ima finally got the idea that maybe Tim wasn't
as excited about her find as she was.

"You're not saying anything. I thought you'd really be excited about these things."

"Why?"

"Because, because they're all about communication!"

"You really think so?" Tim asked flatly.

"Yes. We have really good communication around here. We might have a lot of other problems, but not that. Just look at all the ways we communicate. We use memos, e-mail, Lotus notes, virtual meetings, newsletters, electronic message boards, bulletin boards, and I've probably missed some! We have a lot of other problems in this plant, but communication isn't one of them!"

"You really think all of that is communication?" Tim asked sarcastically.

"Yes. Of course."

"Ima, I'm sorry I snapped at you. But communication — or rather, poor communication — is a pet peeve of mine. *Everyone* thinks he's 'The Great Communicator'! And every organization — ours included — thinks it does such a great job in communicating! But in reality, they fail miserably."

"I beg to disagree," Ima retorted. "We *do* have great communication. And you're looking at the proof right in front of you."

"No. No. And no! This isn't communication. What this is . . . is . . . *advertising!*"

Ima looked down at the "communication. "Advertising? No way!"

"Oh, yes. Tell me. How do *you* define communication?"

Ima let herself ponder the question for a few minutes.

"Communication is talking."

"Uh huh. That's right. Communication is *talking*. Passing information from one person to another. Face to face. With the other person passing information back — at least acknowledging that he understands. It's a two-way process. Take a look at all that stuff. How much of it includes sending and receiving and acknowledging information?"

Ima looked at the stuff lying on the floor. "Well, actually, none of it. But, it's passing information along. And it's so much more efficient! I mean, sending an e-mail is so much quicker and easier than trying to talk to maybe hundreds of people one at a time!"

"Sure it's easier to spread words around like this. Two-way communication takes time and effort! But think about it: What we talk about is what becomes important. Not what we read in an e-mail!"

Ima pondered the idea. Tim could see that she wasn't entirely convinced yet. He tried another tactic. "You have a teenager, don't you, Ima?" he asked. As she nodded, he continued. "When your kid got to the age when he started to go out with his friends at night, I'm sure you gave him a curfew."

Again, Ima nodded.

"Well, when you gave that curfew, you didn't just write it down and slip it under his bedroom door, did you?"

Ima laughed. "Of course not. It was important! I had to talk to him!" Even as she said that, she was startled by her own words. "Oh, yeah!" she said.

"That's right," said Tim. "It was important. So you

talked to him. If you had posted it with a magnet on the refrigerator or slipped it under the door, he could always — and maybe legitimately — say he didn't see it. But when you talked to him face-to-face . . . "

Tim let his words sink in, then he continued, pointing to the "communication" paraphernalia: "There's a place for this *stuff*. I'm not going to deny that. But advertising — one-way communication — should only be a trigger that reminds us about something important. It should never, never try to be the vehicle to learn information or to influence."

"I see that face-to-face communication is important, but the CEO or the vice president can't possibly go out and talk to every employee! That's impossible. Why, our company has thousands of employees!" Ima protested.

"Uh, huh. That's where home-team meetings and the basic building blocks of our foundation come into play."

"What do you mean?"

"Communication in an organization can't be a random event. It has to be *planned* and *executed*. And of course, the process of communication has to be *non-negotiable, focused on business*, done with a sense of *urgency* and with an *accountability* to make it happen. And it all starts in the home-team meeting, which provides the opportunity for face-to-face interactions to occur with regularity."

Ima nodded as she tried to take in what Tim was telling her. He continued: "You're right when you said that the CEO or top leader in the organization couldn't possibly talk to everyone face-to-face. But he actually does talk to everyone, through us, in a 'pass-down' and 'pass-up' system."

What is communication?

In employee surveys, one complaint that employees consistently make is "lack of communication."

Organizations typically respond by putting into place more programs that focus on sharing information and data: newsletters, videos, electronic boards, town-hall meetings and similar things. All of these programs have their place, but they are not communication. And they are not what employees want.

Employees want to hear and to be heard. They want information — but they want to be able to look their bosses in the eye when it is given to them. They want the opportunity to give their opinions and ask questions. And the only way to do that effectively is face-to-face.

Communication is the delivering and receiving of information in a personal, two-way manner. It occurs with the exchange of words that convey meaning, as well as through intonation and body language.

All the other ways of exchanging information are advertising — a one-way method of sharing information that does not assure effective internalization. Advertising has its place, to be sure. Once two-way communication has taken place, the information can be reinforced through various advertising means, such as e-mail, bulletin boards, company newsletters and electronic messaging boards.

No matter how well or graphically sophisticated the delivery, however, advertising is just advertising. It can never take the place of face-to-face exchange.

The primary team defines the non-negotiables of organizational communication. For communication to become ingrained in the organization, it must be process-driven — disciplined, routine, structured and involving everyone in the organization.

The words "pass down" and "pass up" caught Ima's attention. "What do you mean?"

"Every team needs to run their meeting with an agenda — a menu of items to be discussed that is sent out to team members prior to the meeting. Two of the standing agenda items are 'pass up' and 'pass down.' Information that needs to be shared is put into these agenda items and is passed up or down.

"Here's an example: Let's say that the president announces in the primary team meeting that *The Customer* is going to tour the plant next week. He wants to impress on everyone — every worker — that this visit is crucial to the company's getting a huge contract. The president puts 'crucial customer visit next Tuesday' on the pass-down agenda item.

"Now here's the neat thing: Every member on the primary team takes that pass-down item and puts it on their agenda as a pass-down item! The item gets cascaded downward until it reaches every person in the plant — usually within 48 hours. Employees get the pass-down message as if it came directly from the president himself."

Tim let Ima think about that for a minute. "Pass up works the same way," he continued. "When my team broke the all-time departmental safety record for no lost-time accidents last month, I put that accomplishment on the pass-up agenda item. I knew that by putting it on the pass-up agenda, the president would learn about it. He did, and he personally came by to congratulate every team member on the accomplishment."

"Wow! That's pretty cool," said Ima. "I now see that communication must be a two-way process and that these things we've been doing are at best advertising attempts. In addition to pass-up and pass-down, how do we make real communication happen?"

Tim looked her in the eyes. "Just apply the four building blocks and take the first step."

Ima went over to the building blocks and first step they had already constructed and reviewed them.

"Let's see, non-negotiables. This would have to mean that communication — like home-team membership — is a given. It's non-negotiable. It just has to happen. And . . . since home-teams have to happen, the primary way for communication to occur is through the home-team membership!" A light bulb seemed to go off.

"Uh, huh," said Tim. "Keep going. You're doing fine."

Ima outlined the second brick with the tips of her fingers — *business focus.* "This one I'm a little confused about. How does business focus affect communication?"

Tim looked off in the distance to gather his thoughts. "Meetings are not social occasions," he explained, "despite how some people use them. I'm not putting down socialization — everyone needs people. But the primary purpose of the home-team meeting is to convey — through face-to-face exchange — business information and to make sure — through active listening — that this information is understood and accepted . . . that everyone is on the same page concerning making the business successful.

"So to do this, we use an agenda and some other tools. But the written agenda helps make sure we all stay on the same page, so to speak. It's all part of the communication strategy."

Ima nodded. She saw how a business focus tied in with communication. "How do you make communication urgent?"

"Easy," said Tim. "Tone. Attitude. Frequency of meetings — which is established by the primary team. And establishing time frames for accomplishing tasks and reporting back to the team."

Ima touched the home-team step and the accountability block at the same time. "So, people are not only accountable to participate on a home team, they are also accountable to stick to the agenda, do their tasks and report back!"

She stood up abruptly, and walked briskly away from Tim.

"Hey! Where are you going?" he yelled.

"To get the rest of the communication materials. We've got to build our second step — communication — right now!"

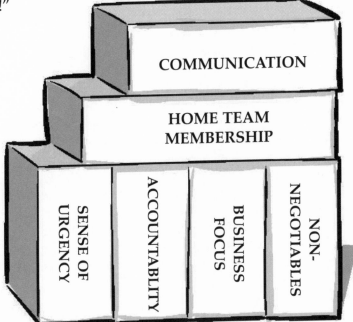

What does it take to make communication happen?

Communication is a two-way street. And in a successful organization, communication is not a random event. It is a planned process, just like any other business function.

When you plan your communication strategy, incorporate these key elements to focus meetings to action, (not endless discussion), enable participation, and provide a consistent flow of information throughout your organization.

• *Minimum frequency.* Since the primary two-way communication vehicle is the home-team meeting, the primary (top) team establishes the minimum frequency standard, based on business cycles and needs. All teams must meet at this minimum frequency to ensure timely communication around the business.

• *Purpose and outcomes.* Define in advance the business purpose and outcomes you desire from your meetings. Specifying the purpose and outcomes of your meetings enables focused preparation and clarity around topics and defines the level of urgency for activities that result from the meeting.

• *Agenda.* Plan every meeting around an agenda, which not only lists the topics to be discussed, but also the time frames in which to discuss them and the person who will lead the discussion/presentation. A structured agenda reinforces the business focus and sense of urgency for communication and action relative to the business topics.

• *Processes for effectiveness.* Determine how the communication should occur. What information needs to be passed up/down to all home teams and by when? What information needs to be brought into the meeting from other home teams? The agenda must include a status update of outstanding actions from the previous meeting as well as a verification of new actions that arise during the meeting so there is complete clarity about who is doing what and when.

• *Roles and responsibilities.* Meetings need a leader, a recorder and a time keeper. These roles must be identified and filled prior to the meeting so that individuals come prepared to fulfill them. Filling these roles makes sure that someone is ready to facilitate the agenda, document actions, capture pass-up/pass-down information and document decision and key discussion points.

For routine, standard meetings a rotation plan for filling these roles among participants ensures that meetings are governed by process and are not dependent on personality.

• *Behavioral parameters.* These are the ground rules for that define acceptable and unacceptable behavior in meetings. Some examples: no interruptions, be on time, respect one another, stay on the topic, everyone participates and cell phones off.

• *Audit process.* The audit process applies a continuous-improvement mindset to the communication strategy. A simple audit is to ask, at the end of each meeting, "What went well during this meeting?" and "What needs to be done to improve the next meeting?"

Always keep in mind that communication only occurs face-to-face. Any other "communication" is advertising, which reinforces and supplements the face-to-face process.

Chapter 6
Keeping Score

They worked steadily, and when they were finished, they stood back and looked at their handiwork:

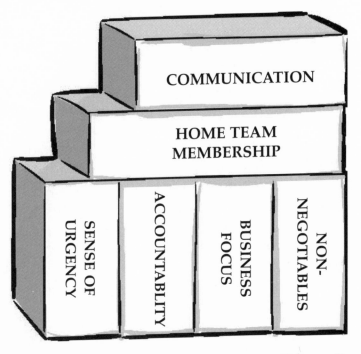

COMMUNICATION

HOME TEAM MEMBERSHIP

SENSE OF URGENCY

ACCOUNTABILITY

BUSINESS FOCUS

NON-NEGOTIABLES

"That was a lot of work!" exclaimed Ima. "I hope I'm up to finishing these steps. I don't think we're ever going to get it done and get out of here."

"It's coming along," said Tim. "Let's get started again."

That said, they went back to their corners and began the arduous task of sorting.

It was tedious work. So much trash had accumulated over the years! And it *was* trash, stuff that had needed to be thrown out, long ago, emptied from this dumpster. Finding the necessary materials to build the steps was a real time-consuming job.

Time ticked on. After a while, Tim began to hear an occasional sob that turned into a whimper and then finally a cry. "Waaa," Ima cried. "We're never going to get out of here."

"Hey! It's going to be all right, Ima. Don't worry, we're really making progress. We're going to get out!"

"No we aren't. We're not getting anywhere." she cried.

"You know what you sound like?" Tim asked with a tinge of impatience in his voice. Ima shook her head and blew her nose. "You sound just like my kids when we take a trip. *'Are we there yet?'* they whine. *'Are we?'"*

Ima wiped her nose. "Yeah, I guess so. I'm sorry. I'll be quiet. My kids do the same thing and they drive me crazy when they do."

"Uh, huh. And how do you handle it when they start whining *'Are we there yet'?"*

She sniffed then answered. "I dunno. I guess I just tell them to be quiet."

"Yeah. That's what I used to do, too. But it didn't do too much good. Because after a few minutes one of them would start in again. Whining. And it drove me crazy! But I finally realized that they kept asking because they were eager to get to our destination, whatever it was. And they were frustrated because they really *didn't* know where we were.

"Well, I decided that the best way to keep them quiet was to give them a way to measure our progress. So I taught them how to read a map and road signs. So when we started our trip, they pinpointed where we were going on the map, how far away it was, and how to measure how far we had gone."

"Did it work?" asked Ima.

"Sure. It not only became a game for them, but it kept them focused."

"I'll have to try it with my kids," Ima responded absently. As she said that, she cocked her head upward. "Hmmm. . . . Measuring progress. I wonder if there is a way to measure *our* progress here?"

She got up and walked to the staircase they were building. Then she went back to her pile of discards and rummaged until she came up with a long flexible tape measure. "Hey! Look what I found. I think we can measure the distance to the top of the wall and calculate how many more steps we'll need. Then we'll be able to actually see our progress and measure it against our goal!"

Tim smiled at her resourcefulness, then he helped her reel out the tape measure and calculate the distance to the top of the wall. Ima noted the measurements on a piece of paper and used her calculator to crunch some numbers.

"Based on the depth and width of the steps we've already built, and assuming that dimensions of the rest of the staircase will be approximately the same, I think we're going to need . . . three more steps. What do you think, Tim?"

"I think you're right, Ima."

"And you know, I think that measuring our progress will help keep me focused and not frustrated."

"Uh, huh," Tim encouraged.

"You know, this isn't too much different from the production goals we set each week. We know exactly how much we have to manufacture. Then, bam! We go for it. Full force. We put everything we have into making those goals. And we almost always do."

"Almost always?" Tim asked.

"Well, yeah. I mean ... we make the production goals, but sometimes QC rejects stuff. They complain that we aren't making spec. And I have to admit that sometimes, not often, we ship product that's, well, kinda marginal. But production comes first and we make the quota!"

"What happens when you ship that marginal product? Any repercussions?"

"Sometimes. We get customer complaints. A lot of them, actually. Of course, I don't talk to the customer myself. It comes down from ABOVE. And I get my wrists slapped."

Tim just looked at her. "So you don't make your customer happy."

"No. . . . "

"Hmmm."

"Oh, come on! Don't be so judgmental. Don't tell me that never happens to you!"

"We're not perfect. It happens. But not very often."

"How come?"

Tim opened his backpack and fumbled in it until he found a notebook. He opened it and gave it to Ima. "We keep score."

Ima took the scorecard from Tim and examined it. It looked similar to the report cards her kids brought home from school. On it, listed vertically, were six items: quality, safety, cost, productivity, people and customer service.

There were columns that said "smart objectives," "target," "owner," "tracking frequency visible indicator," with six months listed beneath this column, and "comments."

Business Scorecard

Key Focus Area	Smart Objectives	target	owner	Tracking frequency visible indicator*						Comments
				Jan	Feb	Mar	Apr	May	Jun	
Quality										
Safety										
Cost										
Productivity										
People										
Customer Service										
*Can be quarterly, monthly, weekly or daily as appropriate										

"Obviously this is some kind of goals sheet," commented Ima. "I understand the productivity goal. But I don't understand why those other things are listed on your scorecard. Other people are responsible for those things. I mean, like quality. That's the responsibility of quality control. And safety. I know we have to work safely, but safety goals are for the safety director. And the one I really can't understand is people. Isn't that for human resources? I would think so. That's *their* business."

"Hmmm. You think so? It seems to me that these six items — quality, safety, cost, productivity, people and customer service — are key business focus areas and that they pertain to every team and every individual in the company. From the primary team and the president on down to the janitor ... Sure ... the specific accountability — how the goals are achieved — will vary according to the team and the person. But think about it. Isn't everyone accountable for these six things? "

Ima considered what Tim was saying.

"This scorecard keeps us focused," Tim continued. "And it keeps us balanced. We don't just produce our quota without regard for these other things, because if we did, something would get out of kilter. Like safety. If we just aimed for a production goal without regard for safety, people could get hurt. And if that happened, costs would go out of balance. And so would our people goals, because then we might have to hire someone new and train them."

Tim saw that Ima was still a little confused. "Let me explain it another way. Let's say we have a goal to increase production by 20%. It would be easy to do this with expensive new equipment, but that would defeat the purpose. So we might have a goal of increasing production without increasing current costs — a cost goal. And we could do this by cutting scrap and waste by 10% — a quality goal. And by reducing workers' comp costs by 15% — a safety goal. And to achieve those goals, we would train and develop our workers in teamwork, orientation and safety procedures — a people goal.

"So, you see, all of these things work together in tandem," explained Tim. "Whatever project we're working on, we work on it with all of these key processes in mind. We don't neglect one area for the sake of another. And that's why my team almost always makes its production goals and rarely gets customer complaints."

Ima held the scorecard up to Tim. "This scorecard, can I keep it? It seems to have all the elements on it to incorporate our four foundation blocks: non-negotiables, business focus, a sense of urgency and accountability. And it also builds on the two steps that we already have in place — home-team membership and communication. You don't suppose—"

"Yes, I suppose!" Tim said.

And with that, the two of them attacked the task at hand — building the third step that would lead them out of the dumpster.

Business Scorecards

A business scorecard is a simple and concise tracking mechanism that allows the team to monitor and respond to key business metrics. Its purpose is to provide a clear and concise business focus for each team and to drive the direct lines of accountability for each team's business contributions.

- The scorecard itself is non-negotiable. Each team must use one. The primary team designs a standard format to ensure consistent understanding throughout the organization.
- The primary team develops the global scorecard. Using the key business-focus areas, the primary team designs the global scorecard, which measures overall organizational performance.

The global scorecard's specific objectives are high-level and are supported by the objectives incorporated on scorecards at other organizational levels. The primary team reviews the global scorecard weekly during its team meeting. The rest of the organization reviews the global scorecard monthly during a home-team meeting.

- The scorecard lists objectives for each business-focus area. Each objective must meet SMART criteria — Specific, Measurable, Achievable, Relevant and Timely. Using SMART criteria for objectives ensures the team has written an effective objective

Once the global scorecard is complete, teams begin to develop scorecards specifically defining how they support the global scorecard. Each team must have a minimum of one objective for each key business-focus area. Teams can add key business-focus areas. They cannot, however, take away from the key focus areas.

Scorecard development cascades throughout all organizational levels until every team in the organization has a scorecard with specific metrics for each key business-focus area that reflects the team's performance.

- The scorecard is reviewed in all home-team meetings. A standing agenda item for each home-team meeting is a scorecard review. During discussion, the team identifies best practices to share for performance above targets, and develops corrective action plans for performance below target. Reviewing and discussing scorecards gives home-team meetings a sense of urgency.

• The scorecard reinforces accountability in several ways. First, by listing performance targets for each objective. As objectives are routinely (typically weekly, monthly or quarterly) tracked, results are compared against these targets to gauge team performance.

Second, by identifying owners of the objectives. The objective owner is not responsible for accomplishing the objective. Rather, this team member is responsible for updating the scorecard prior to each meeting to make sure the scorecard is accurate.

Third, by using visible indicators to quickly set the tone of the home team meeting. The visible indicator is a way to see at a glance if the objective is being met.

For example, a visible indicator could be a color — a red, yellow or green — to describe performance. Red would indicate that performance is not meeting a target, green that objective performance is meeting a target, and yellow would indicate a trend from red to green or green to red.

These visible indicators allow the team to look at the scorecard and in five seconds diagnose the overall status of team performance. If the teams sees a lot of green indicators, team performance is good and the tone of the meeting will be positive. If the team sees a lot of red indicators, team performance is poor and the meeting will be focused on developing corrective action plans to improve performance.

• Teams routinely share scorecards with senior management. Teams send their scorecards with corresponding corrective action plans to senior managers monthly for review. Many organizations replace reviews with monthly presentations. In these presentations, teams at all levels present their business performance to senior leaders. A scorecard clearly demonstrating how a team is contributing to the business makes a very powerful statement. It's process-based leadership in action.

Chapter 7
You're It!

When Tim and Ima finished smoothing the surface of the third step, Ima admired their handiwork. "There's certainly something to be said about measuring progress. Look, we're 60 percent done!"

Tim agreed. "Yep. But being 60 percent done means that we still have 40 percent to go if we want to get out of here. So, what do you think the next step has to be, Ima?"

Ima climbed down the steps and walked around the base of the staircase, reviewing each of the foundation blocks.

NON-NEGOTIABLES
BUSINESS FOCUS
SENSE OF URGENCY
ACCOUNTABILITY

It was good, she thought, that they had used four foundation stones. They were carrying a lot of weight.

Then she re-climbed **Step One: Home-Team Membership.** Yes, she thought. That was essential. That was where all the direction, communication and focus came from.

Step Two was **Communication.** You couldn't break out of any dumpster without good two-way, face-to-face communication, she thought. And now she understood that communication was much, much more than e-mails, memos, bulletin boards and newsletters.

And **Step Three** — the one they just finished — was **Business Scorecards.** That step really would keep the team aimed at the right work with ever-present regard for the work of the total organization, not just production, she believed.

She walked back down the steps and sat next to Tim. "I don't know. We've covered a lot. If I had been managing with *just* these processes all along, I probably wouldn't be in this fix right now! But obviously it's not enough to get us — me — out of here. But I just don't know what the next step should be."

"Let's look at it a different way," said Tim. "If you could build any step — do anything — to get out of this dumpster, what would it be?"

Ima sat hunched over, her elbows on her knees, her hands holding her head up. She sat deep in thought and was silent for several minutes. Finally she said, "I get so tired of *doing* everything. I mean, my team is really good at problem solving, like I already told you. Give them a problem and boy! They can come up with a solution. But when it comes to getting the projects done and everyone has to do a little more work, well, that's a different story. It's like that situation I told you about with Monk and our last team meeting. We were all set to fix the problem, then Monk refused to take responsibility. And the whole thing got postponed.

"And that's just one example. It's a lot of other things, too. Everyone expects me to get everything done. From getting their safety glasses and gloves, to ordering regular supplies, to completing reports, to fixing shorted paychecks! *I'm* supposed to do it all! My days get longer and I'm not even able to get the work done that I really think needs to be done, like planning and making it easier to achieve our goals.

"So, I guess if I could build a step — any step — to get me out of here, it would be *to get people to stop dumping on me!*"

Tim paraphrased Ima's wish: "So you think that if people took responsibility themselves to get things done, they wouldn't dump on you."

Ima nodded in accord.

"That personal accountability thing is really tough," Tim said. "I remember a problem-solving meeting of a group of supervisors I once observed . . . "

He proceeded to describe the meeting to Ima. The company had been going through some tough times, and it decided an all-out makeover was needed. Top management was convinced that employees had to become more involved with their work, so it put into place new processes, similar to the steps that Ima and Tim were building.

Everything was going well, except in one of the key assembly departments. There, communication was breaking down between shifts, employees were becoming frustrated, and productivity and quality were in the basement. The whole employee-involvement process stopped cold.

The superintendent rounded up all of the supervisors and demanded, "You're going to go into that conference room and work out what's wrong. Don't come out until you have a solution!"

The eight supervisors took their coffee cups and a

box of donuts and locked themselves in the meeting room. For the first two hours, all they did was complain. They took no responsibility for their actions:

"I don't know why we have to do this. It's those workers who won't do what they're told! They just won't come to problem-solving meetings."

"It's not my fault quality fell. They beefed up the specifications and employees didn't do what they were supposed to do."

"If only 'management' would get its act together." (The supervisors failed to recognize that they were part of management!)

"This new structure is just another 'flavor of the month' program. It'll never work."

The griping went on and on. The supervisors didn't seem to be making any progress on finding a solution to their productivity, quality and communication problems. Around lunch time, one of the more timid supervisors said, almost in a whisper, *"Maybe it's us."*

The two colleagues sitting next to him raised their eyebrows at his comment, but ignored him. They just joined in the complaining for another 30 minutes. But the timid supervisor no longer participated. He eventually got up to get a cup of coffee and retreated to a corner of the room, away from the others. He just sat, peered into the dark coffee in his cup and listened.

His co-workers finally fell silent when they realized that he was no longer "with" them. They asked, "What's the matter with you?"

He shook his head. "I think we're wrong. It's not *them*. Oh, sure. We can point fingers at a lot of people.

But if we want to make changes in our productivity and quality, then the burden is on our shoulders. *It's us.* If we want to fix this problem, we have to take the first step. We have to accept the responsibility and hold our employees accountable to do what they are supposed to do. It may not be fun, but it's our job!"

His cohorts looked at him as if he were some type of outcast. Finally, one of them said, "I think he's right. I'm willing to do it."

And eventually all of the supervisors came around to owning up to their accountability. By the end of the day, they made a pact and acted together. That department never had a productivity or quality problem again.

"You actually saw this happen?" Ima asked.

"Well," admitted Tim, "I was a little more than an observer. I was the quiet supervisor. And that was the day I took my first real step at climbing out of my dumpster. I confronted the truth. And I confronted my colleagues."

Ima considered the moral of Tim's story. "So, if I understand you correctly, if I want my employees to take more responsibility, I have to take the first step. I have to take the responsibility to stop the dumping!"

"That's right."

"That's tough. How do I do it?" Ima wondered.

"The tough part comes from inside — summoning up the courage to confront. Once you gather those inner resources — and I know you have them — then it's not too hard. It's actually a pretty simple process."

Tim continued, "When someone — like Monk — tries to dump on you, discuss the dumping issue with him. *Then tell him he is responsible for solving his own problem.*

When you give that responsibility, you also have to give him resources — tools — to fix it. And then — very important — you have to follow up. Too often that's where we fail," said Tim.

Ima laughed. "Yeah. I remember years ago, I had a job in an office. One of my monthly tasks was to prepare a pretty detailed report. I did that for more than a year. One day, I asked my supervisor if she ever got any feedback on the report. She shrugged her shoulders and admitted she never did. Well, the next month, we had a crisis, and I was overloaded with work. For the first time ever, I simply forgot to do the report. I didn't remember it until the following month. And even though I remembered it that month, I was still so overloaded, that I deliberately chose not to do it. Two months, no report. And no one ever asked about it. *No one ever followed up to find out if I had done it.* I finally just stopped doing it altogether. I guess it wasn't important after all, because my supervisor never followed up on it."

"That's exactly what happens, Ima. If we don't show our employees that something is important by our actions, then our employees believe — rightfully — that it is not important. So they won't do it. Why should they? But if we follow up, we let them know it is important.

"But to get back to the process, if you find out that the employee has taken care of the problem, all you have to do is make a note of it. But if he's not done it and needs you to remove some barriers — like make some calls or give him some tools — then you do your part and expect him to get his part done. Following up is critical to making people take responsibility."

You have the power to stop the dumping

Here's the process to use:

1. Identify and discuss the dumping issues. When an employee brings you a problem, discuss it to identify who should solve it. It might surprise you that most problems don't need your "expert" intervention. Employees can solve them themselves, provided you give them the tools to do so.

2. Assign the responsibility. If your employee can solve the problem, make her responsible for it. Of course, make sure she has the knowledge and resources to solve it. If she doesn't, clearly define what she needs to do to solve the problem. Take responsibility for those tasks she doesn't have the resources to complete, pair up on those tasks she doesn't have the knowledge to complete (and teach her) and allow her to do those tasks she has the skills and knowledge to do.

3. Follow up. When you do, you'll find one of three things:

• The employee carried out his responsibility and solved the problem. Nothing more is required from you or him.

• The employee has run into some problems. She needs your help to remove barriers. For example — she needs your signature to authorize her to purchase supplies. Provide the appropriate support and then let her solve the problem. Establish a new follow-up time to make sure she has done her part.

• The employee did nothing. This is where most managers drop the ball. If you let the employee do nothing, you have allowed yourself to become a dumpster again. Instead, if the employee does nothing, give him a new deadline and tell him it is part of his job to complete the action. Not completing the action may be a performance issue. If the problem is more personal in nature (for example — the employee's paycheck is wrong and he chooses not to get it corrected), it is the employee's issue — not yours. It's not your problem to solve!

The hardest part in stopping employees from dumping on you is following through — don't let the employee off the hook. Remember: Your job is not to solve all of your employees' problems. Your job is to enable them to solve their problems. This is true empowerment.

Ima looked worried. "All that following up. How do you do it? How do you keep track of all these de-dumping projects?"

Tim reached for his knapsack again and took out a tablet of forms. "I use this," he said. He handed the tablet to Ima.

"Hey, this is a pretty neat tool!" exclaimed Ima. "I mean, it lets you document problems and actions and make comments. If I were to use this, if Monk, or anyone else, failed to follow through on his part, I would have a handy-dandy reference guide. I wouldn't have to rely on my memory, which I admit, can sometimes let me down!"

"That's the whole point of this Action Register, Ima. It keeps you on track and it keeps the employee on track, too. When I'm dealing with an employee, I actually complete this register in duplicate! I fill it out and give a copy to my employee. That way, he has a written record of what's he's supposed to do. There can be no misunderstanding about the communication that takes place between him and me. It's a great tool. And you know how else I use it?" Ima shook her head. "Performance management!"

Because Tim had been completing appraisal forms at

Action Register

ACTION	RESPONSIBILITY	TARGET	COMPLETE	COMMENTS

home the night before, he had several in his knapsack, along with sheaves of Action Registers. He handed a set to Ima to look at.

"Wow!" said Ima. "These Action Registers make completing performance appraisal forms a snap," said Ima. "All you have to do is look through these forms. You've got a written record of all the good and the not-so-good. It's all very explicit. So it doesn't take you too long to fill out the forms. And these Action Registers let you be very specific. It's all documented. *I like this!* If I had these to complete my employees' performance appraisals, I don't think I would dread doing them so much."

"That's right," said Tim. "The annual performance appraisal becomes a mere formality, because you've been communicating with your employees and documenting your communication through the registers. You look at the registers, analyze patterns of behavior and performance and identify areas in which to help develop your employees. And you can also spot the things you should formally commend in the appraisal," said Tim.

"But don't confuse *performance appraisals* with performance management," he emphasized.

Ima looked at him confused. "I don't understand. Isn't performance management the same thing as performance appraisal?"

"Uh, uh," Tim shook his head. "Performance appraisal is actually just that annual or semi-annual event of sitting down with your employees and formally going over documentation about their performance. What happens, though, is that if pay raises are tied to the performance appraisal, employees don't hear what you want them to hear. All they want to know is 'How much do I get?'

"Performance *management,* however, is actually managing performance to help employees make incremental changes in outputs and behavior. So, when you manage performance, you give appropriate feedback in a timely manner. The process involves rewarding and acknowledging good performance, identifying and rectifying deficient performance and applying consequences to unchanged behavior and performance."

"Hmmm . . . that makes sense. People work every day, so performance is ongoing, not a once-a-year thing. It makes sense that feedback should be ongoing. And the register, by its design, would force me to make feedback ongoing. The long shot of this is, that makes everyone accountable — including me!"

Ima, deep in thought, leafed through the Action Registers Tim had maintained for one of his employees. "It seems to me that there are different levels or kinds of accountability. I mean, the most important, of course, is personal accountability. Every individual has to be accountable to do 'his thing.' But the first non-negotiable item — step — is that everyone has to participate on a home team. How do we hold the team accountable to do what it says it is going to do?"

Tim allowed himself a small smile when he heard Ima use the word "we." She was buying into the accountability processes, he thought. Out loud, he said, "Let's look at the Business Scorecard again."

Tim and Ima looked at the Business Scorecard form. He explained, "Remember that we said the team sets SMART objectives for each of the key focus areas?"

Ima nodded.

"Well, setting objectives is just the first step. Once an objective is set, the team has to develop an action plan — an Action Register — outlining how to achieve the objective and who will be responsible for the several tasks involved in working toward it. Then, at each team meeting,

---

What Is Performance Management?

Do you dread doing performance appraisals? If you do, you aren't alone. Most managers dread doing them because they don't have good data sources from which to draw information. Most employees go into an appraisal with the assumption that if they have heard nothing, they must be doing ok. Many employees experience anxiety before a performance appraisal because they really don't know what the appraisal is going to reflect.

Performance appraisal as a stand-alone event doesn't work. What does work, however, is performance management.

Performance appraisal is a formal annual or semi-annual event in which the manager sits down with the employee and discusses past performance, with an eye to the future.

Performance management, on the other hand, is an ongoing process to manage performance. The manager maintains documentation and dialogue with the employee in a continuous effort to change work behaviors and outputs. The performance-management process involves rewarding and acknowledging good performance, identifying and rectifying deficient performance and applying consequences to unchanged behavior and performance.

Performance appraisals are often components of a performance management system, becoming a summary of continuous performance feedback.

---

the team has to report on reaching the objectives and post progress. That progress report — the tracking indicator — should be a visible sign, like a plus sign or a color — red or green. It may also be a metric, such as a percentage completed.

"The Action Register and the visible tracking indicator are two more ways to develop accountability. And in addition to that, a visible tracking indicator shows that the team has fallen behind by failing to achieve its target, the team has to develop an additional action plan."

Ima listened, trying to grasp the nuances of the chart. Tim continued, "This might be clearer to you with an example. Here — take a look at this."

Tim pulled out a Business Scorecard that showed an

Business Scorecard

Key Focus Area	Smart Objectives	target	owner	Tracking frequency visible indicator*						Comments
				Jan	Feb	Mar	Apr	May	Jun	
Quality										
Safety										
Cost										
Productivity										
People										
Customer Service										
*Can be quarterly, monthly, weekly or daily as appropriate										

objective for the key focus area of cost.

"You'll notice that Amy is the 'owner' of this objective. She is not responsible for accomplishing the objective; she is responsible for tracking it for the home team. The home team develops an action plan to accomplish the objective. They capture this action plan on the Action Register form."

Ima was so excited by what she was learning, she paraphrased what Tim had just told her. "Ah, I see! For each SMART objective, the team develops an action plan, which it outlines on this register. And the person who is responsible for executing that step in the action plan is listed on the register. Clever!"

"Clever and efficient," said Tim. "Everybody on the team knows what is expected of him or her. And the 'owner' of the SMART objective knows who to follow up with to update the scorecard. It sounds a little involved, but believe me, it really works. Here, take a look at this Scorecard Action Register that my group developed to accomplish its cost objective of reducing scrap from 3% to 1% by the end of the first quarter."

Tim showed Ima a partially completed register.

Ima spent several minutes reviewing the Scorecard Action Register and mulling over its implications. "You know what I think, Tim? I think that by using the scorecard we keep focused on the business. The personal Action Register holds individuals accountable and stops them from dumping on me! The team Action Register creates accountability to make sure the team's goals and objectives are met.

"It seems to me that these registers could be used in

Business Scorecard

Key Focus Area	Smart Objectives	target	owner	Tracking frequency visible indicator*						Comments
				Jan	Feb	Mar	Apr	May	Jun	
Cost	Reduce scrap from current 3% level to 1% by end of 1st quarter.	Scrap level	Amy	☺ 2.25	☹ 3.125					

another way, too. They could be used to track meeting action items. I mean, not everything that is decided in a meeting requires a complete plan, but there are action items, even if they are only administrative. So, in each meeting you could use an Action Register. There would be no misunderstandings about who is to do what."

Tim smiled at Ima's insights.

She continued, "And you know what else? When people do what they say they will do, then everybody begins to trust each other. I hate to admit it, but trust has been an issue in my team. There have been so many broken promises over the years. Everybody has gotten real good at pointing fingers. But now the finger-pointing stops. The registers and the scorecard spell out responsibilities. This is a really good thing. It will take time, but these tools will help us rebuild trust. And when we become trustworthy, every other process will improve."

Tim smiled at Ima. "So, Ima, what do you think the next step is."

"It's as clear as can be: The next step — *and it's a BIG one* — is **Action Registers. Every team must create,**

Action Register

Objective: Beginning Jan 1, reduce scrap from current 3% level to 1% by end of 1st quarter.

ACTION	RESPONSIBILITY	TARGET	COMPLETED	COMMENTS
Verify equipment specifications and calibration with maintenance	Harvey	January 5	January 5	Completed. Calibration set to standard.
Assess technical training needs for team members	Mary	January 15		Assessment tool completed and passed out January 7. Will compile results and report to team by target
Identify cause of scrap	Jim	January 15	January 15	Long changeover time is resulting in scrap.

monitor and utilize Action Registers in all home-team meetings and with all scorecard items that fall below target. Every team should also use Action Registers to develop and track personal accountability. We certainly have enough building material. Let's do it!"

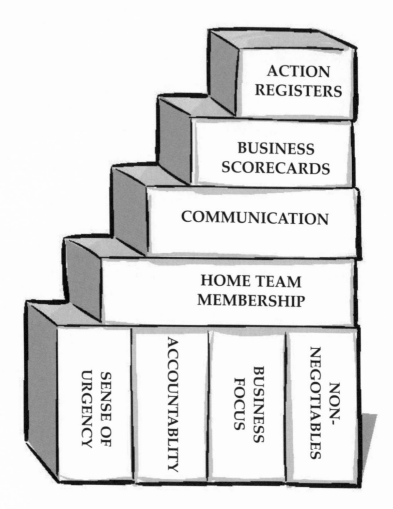

Using an Action Register

It's one thing to tell an employee he is accountable for an action. It's another thing for the employee to feel accountable. Action Registers help develop accountability in employees. They:

- **Help you stop employees from dumping on you.** You can use an Action Register to note a problem an employee brings to you, along with the action the employee — and you, if necessary — will take to resolve it. Then you use the register to follow up and follow through.

- **Contribute to meeting effectiveness.** A meeting Action Register documents action items that result from team meetings. Because individual accountability is identified, there can be no misunderstanding about who is to do what for the meeting and when it will be done. Meetings begin with an Action Register review of items that should have been completed for that meeting and end with an Action Register review of new items identified during the meeting, verification of person responsible for keeping score and target completion dates.

- **Enhance the use of the Business Scorecard.** An Action Register details corrective action plans the team and its members need to take to improve performance on objectives that are not performing to target.

- **Help you manage performance.** When you counsel with employees — including when you administer a formal appraisal — you have in hand documentation of performance. You can quickly identify the number and significance of actions an employee has taken and whether or not he or she consistently makes target completion dates. You can be specific and constructive in developing employee performance.

- **Build trust between you, your employees** and top management. With no more finger-pointing and a true accountability, individuals learn to trust each other to make their commitments. Top managers can review action registers and acknowledge those teams who are truly contributing to business performance.

To use Action Registers effectively, follow these steps:
1. Be specific. Each action item must be detailed enough

so that anyone reviewing the register a year from now will understand the action. Don't write to the fill the box; write to describe the action.

2. Always designate one person who is ultimately accountable. Sometimes several individuals are involved in an action. List all the names, but name one person who has to make "it" happen.

3. Use specific dates. Never use ASAP or other acronyms. These mean different things to different people. As soon as possible may mean by the end of the day to one team member and by the end of next week to another.

4. Never erase renegotiated dates. Merely mark through them so that you can see a history and trends. You'll use these in performance management.

5. State the completion date. This clearly documents when the action was completed and shows which employees get the job done and get it done within their committed times.

6. Renegotiate a new target completion date prior to due date. Inform the employee that if conditions change and he cannot complete the task by the due date, it is his responsibility to bring it to your attention and renegotiate a new date prior to the meeting. This is critical so that team members with actions contingent upon those of that employee can modify their target completion dates accordingly.

7. Archive the team Action Registers. Registers can be maintained electronically or in a handbook maintained by the team. (More on a team handbook in Chapter 8.)

8. Never assign an action to someone who is absent. An individual cannot be held accountable for completing an action he has no say in accepting.

9. Develop an action plan for any item on the scorecard that is not on target. The idea is that registers are more than documentation — they are tools to help your team perform more effectively. Teams should document the specific steps they will take to improve business performance reflected on their scorecard. If you don't use Action Registers to drive corrective action plans for scorecards, scorecards become more of a tracking tool instead of a tool to drive a clear and concise business focus and your employees lose a sense of urgency and accountability!

Chapter 8
Book It!

"Whew!" exclaimed Ima as she and Tim put the last pieces into place. "Step 4 was really a lot of work." She wiped perspiration off her brow.

"Let's go back and rest for a few minutes," said Tim. "We deserve it."

They carefully walked down the steep steps to the bottom of the trash pile and sat down to relax for a moment. Ima gazed up toward their handiwork and the top of the dumpster. "We've done a lot. We're almost there. Just one . . . more . . . step . . . " She enunciated the words slowly and let their reality sink in. "One more. It's going to be *so good* to get out of here! And when I do get out of here, it's going to be so different. No more dumping! I feel liberated already. I'm even eager to participate on *my* home team — and I've never been fond of meetings!"

Tim leaned back on a large stack of memos that they had already gone through. He didn't say anything. He was enjoying watching Ima grow and learn.

Ima suddenly snapped out of her reverie. She pulled her knees up and hugged herself tightly. Her expression changed so abruptly from elation to fear that Tim became alarmed.

"Ima, you're as white as a ghost. What happened? A second ago you were on Cloud 9. Now?"

"Oh, Tim. Something just occurred to me and it really scared me. I'm almost as scared as when we fell into this place this morning. Here we are, almost out of here. And when we get out, it's going to be good. I know it is! I should be happy! I was happy. Because I know I can do this. I can work with my employees and put process-based leadership in place. But, Tim, what happens if we get a new vice president? Or what happens if my team changes? Or if I get promoted or switched to another department? It could happen all over again. I could fall into this dumpster and be buried alive. All over again."

"What makes you think that will happen?" asked Tim.

"It's happened before. And history always repeats itself."

Ima recounted one of the disasters she had lived through — a supervisory training program. "It happened years ago when I was a new supervisor here," Ima remembered.

The Eniware plant was a few years old and rapidly expanding. Its workforce was growing by several hundred employees a year as the popularity of its products exploded. But like any other business that has experienced rapid expansion, Eniware had its share of growing pains. Some of the worst of those pains came about as a result of inexperienced first-level managers. Most had been promoted from the ranks. And while they were technically proficient, they lacked leadership skills.

"Management decided the plant needed supervisory training," Ima recalled. "So, it hired a training manager who investigated several popular training programs. Each of the venders gave a presentation to the training manager and top management, and with the training manager's recommendation, they spent a small fortune on a program that put every manager through two full weeks of training, which was heavily concentrated on problem solving and communication skills."

Every single supervisor and manager in the plant "earned" a certificate, explained Ima. The plant manager was fully behind the program and expected miracles to happen.

"Things went well for awhile," she said. "It wasn't perfect around here, but at least we supervisors felt we knew a little bit more about managing than we did before the training. But about 18 months later, the economy turned and we had to lay off some employees — including the training manager. I guess they decided that training was one of those things that could 'go' when things were tight."

"What happened then?" asked Tim.

"Well, there was no more training — either for supervisors or more employees. Since we weren't hiring anybody, that wasn't too bad. But as you know, recessions don't last forever, and we snapped out of that one in about nine months. We recalled employees and hired new ones. We even hired some new supervisors. But because we didn't have a training manager, no one got the training they needed. I mean, even old employees needed refresher training. They had been off work for months! And new supervisors didn't get trained either. People started to do their 'own thing.' Consistency went by the wayside."

"Give me an example," said Tim.

"Hmmm . . . like attendance policies. We began to see some inconsistencies and unfairness. A few supervisors would do things like let their favorite people leave early, or would look the other way when some people came in late, but stick to the rules when people they didn't like did. Things like that started to cause morale problems. Although we had been taught supervisory skills in our earlier training, the training wasn't being put to use any longer.

"Well, management finally decided it was time to hire another training manager, so they recruited a guy who had made his mark with a competitor. This fellow came in, took a look at the training program that we used earlier and declared that it was passé. Instead of making a unilateral decision about what was good for us, though, he created a training committee. I was asked to participate on it, along with some other first-line supervisors and some managers from operations and support areas, like quality control and maintenance."

Ima paused for a few minutes to gather her thoughts. "We brainstormed a lot and finally came up with a list of things we felt everyone — including our employees — should be trained on. The new training manager then bought a variety of off-the-shelf programs and started putting everyone through them."

"And?" encouraged Tim.

"The training manager — and top management — seemed to be more concerned that everybody went through the training programs than they were that any-one learned anything. People went to the programs, but no one used the skills and knowledge they learned. When they came back from training, they just did what they had always done before.

"As you might expect, with everyone doing his own thing — including enforcing policies — quality started to deteriorate and productivity went down. That obviously was a problem. So the next thing the plant manager decided to do was to hire a quality director, who in turn decided we had to have total quality management — TQM — throughout the organization."

Ima idly stacked manila folders as she talked. "Again we all went through training. But this time, the emphasis was on maintaining quality — not actually on supervisory skills. Sometimes the TQM stuff seemed to conflict with stuff we had learned in other programs. Again, very confusing. But we plugged on . . .

"Until, and you may remember this — I think you had been hired by then — the company president was fired and we got a new one. This guy had a reputation for ruthlessly turning companies around."

"Yeah, I remember," said Tim. "The new president scrapped TQM and decided that every plant — including the Eniware plant — had to put in place a 'zero defect' program."

"Zero defects was similar to TQM in a lot of ways," said Ima. "But it was different, too, especially in the language it used. I guess the goals were the same. But, man! It was back to square one again.

"I can deal with the cynicism of my employees — I mean, it's like we talked about earlier — not accepting bad behavior — but what if management changes? Or I'm transferred? Or my team changes? It'll be like those other programs all over again. I just don't want this to be another 'flavor-of-the-month' program."

Ima was clearly depressed and concerned.

Tim sat down in front of her, took her hand and looked her straight in the eye. "Ima, it won't happen. I promise you it won't. But I know you need some guarantees to help you get over your own skepticism. I think — no, I know — that the guarantees you are seeking are the materials you need for the last step."

Ima relaxed just a bit and looked deeply into Tim's eyes to see if he was genuine. He was. "Tim, you've brought me this far. I trust you when you say the answers are here. I'm scared. But I'm even more frightened not to get out of here. I guess I have to give this a try. So let's get back to work and find those building materials. It's just one more step."

Tim offered his hand to help Ima up. During their previous work, they had concentrated on only two of the corners of the dumpster. This time they each went to a different corner where they had not yet looked for material. These areas were still in shambles.

Ima plopped down on a pile of papers and began to sort, again not knowing exactly what she was looking for, but trusting that she would find it, as they had already done so many times today.

"At least I'm learning some organization skills," she mused as she separated memos from e-mails and reports from spread sheets. She dug for a while, and eventually came across a box of three-ring binders.

Curious, she picked one up. It was labeled, "Quality procedures." Putting it aside, she selected another it. It read, "Supervisory policies." And another said, "Complaint procedures." Along with the binders, there were several steno pads labeled: "Meeting minutes."

She threw each of these binders into the trash heap. But after a moment, she reconsidered and went back to the trashcan and pulled them out. "Hmmm, I wonder," she whispered almost inaudibly.

"Did you say something, Ima?" asked Tim, who was also busy going through piles of paper, some white boards, flip charts and easels.

"Hmmm? Oh, I was just thinking. These binders and notebooks, they are giving me an idea. Maybe some sort of documentation could help," Ima said tentatively.

Tim joined Ima. He pulled open a few of the notebooks and said, "I think you might be on to something." He walked back to the white board he had found and brought it back to where Ima was gazing at the notebooks, still deep in thought.

"It's often better to think out loud, Ima. Here, let's do some brainstorming. I'll capture our ideas on the white board. What kind of documentation are you thinking about?" he asked.

Ima screwed up her forehead in thought. "I'm not sure. A few years ago I was involved in a women's business club. To keep the meeting running in an orderly fashion, they followed *Robert's Rules of Order.* I always thought those *Rules* were pretty hokey, but now I see how they served a purpose. They were procedures. And they assured consistency. I mean, every year the club membership changed. And every year, the leadership changed. But the club's purpose and direction and momentum continued. *Robert's Rules of Order* was like a Bible or a handbook for the club.

"In addition to the *Rules of Order,* the club also had a charter and written procedures. At each meeting, the secretary kept minutes. These minutes served as a history and also kept everyone on their toes, because they were a public record of what the club had agreed to do.

Ima leafed through one of the steno pads and one of the three-ring binders labeled "procedures."

"What I'm thinking," she said, "is that we have to have some sort of team handbook, a kind of team rules of order. This handbook would outline the business processes that each team develops. What do you think, Tim?"

Tim had been capturing Ima's ideas on the white board. He stood back and looked at what he had written down:

Handbook:

Gives order to meeting

Focuses on purpose

Outlines procedures

Provides consistency

Serves as a history

Is a public record

"This looks good, Ima. Real good. Now tell me, how do you think you would use such a handbook?"

"Hmmm. I think we could — and should — use it in several ways. For one thing, we could use it for orientation. Boy! I sure wish I had had a team handbook when I was a new employee. My orientation was really bad."

Tim wrote ORIENTATION on the white board and said, "Uh huh. I think each of us has some orientation war stories. My worst experience was my first job out of school. I was hired and told to report to work the next day. I showed up and met my supervisor and two other guys who had been hired. The supervisor said, 'Here's your safety glasses. You get a half-hour lunch at noon. And there is your work station. Ask Toni if you have any questions.' Unfortunately, he didn't bother to tell us who Toni was. I assumed Tony was a guy. Turned out Toni was a woman. I didn't have any idea of what I was doing, but somehow I made it through the day. Not a good experience; not at all. And it didn't give me a good feeling about the company or how much it cared about me and my success."

Ima nodded. "I had a similar experience — more than once. I think I've done a better job at orienting new employees than that. But I admit, not a heck of lot better. My orientations have generally concentrated on work rules and introducing the new person to his nearest co-worker. But I never bothered to tell them about the company or how decisions were made or anything like that.

"But if we had a handbook, well, it could outline the home-team structure. It could state the non-negotiables — so there could be no misunderstanding of expectations. And it could show a new employee the status on our business goals and objectives, because it would con-

tain our Business Scorecard. It would be a breeze to wel-
come him the right way! And, I think a handbook could
also be used for training," said Ima.

Tim wrote down TRAINING on the white board.
"Tell me more about how you see a handbook being
used for training," he said.

"We could have a section in it that details the responsibilities and procedures for all of the jobs in the group,"
said Ima. "It could even be written much like a checklist
— nothing too complicated or sophisticated — just easy
to understand so that, again, there would be no misunderstanding about expectations. I realize, of course, that
you can't just hand the person the book and say, 'Here,
read this and do your job!' That wouldn't be training. But
it would be a reference tool for him and a guidebook for
me. In fact, it just occurred to me that I wouldn't have to
do all of the training myself, because I would know that
the training would follow the outlined procedures."

Ima allowed herself to think through the implications
of having a good training tool and being able to delegate
training. "Training is another area where I've had some
bad experiences. When I've been too busy to train a
newcomer myself, I've always assigned him or her to a
'buddy' — usually one of the most senior people in the
department. I've always assumed that old-timers had to
be the best trainers. But what I found out — the hard
way — is that seniority doesn't necessarily guarantee
good training."

"Did you have a bad experience?" asked Tim.

"That's an understatement," replied Ima. "I'll never
forget the time I put an 'older' worker in charge of train-

ing newcomers on a certain power press. I found out later that the 'training' consisted of saying, 'Here's the on and off switch. Put the parts in here and take them out there.' She neglected to show and tell and check the newcomer on how to set up the safety guards on the machine. Well, the new employee was feeding parts into the machine when suddenly it jammed. The guard was not set up correctly and when she instinctively reached into the machine to unjam it, the press came down on her hand." Ima's face saddened with the memory and her eyes welled up with tears. "She lost the tips of two fingers. We all learned an invaluable lesson. Unfortunately, that employee will be reminded of it all her life, all because I assumed that the senior employee knew how to train. Boy was I wrong."

"That's a tragic story, Ima. I'm so sorry that happened to you," Tim sympathized. "Senior people often know their jobs so well that they don't remember the simple steps. They're too close to their work. And they've often learned to take short-cuts — not always the best thing to do — that they pass on to the unsuspecting new worker."

"Yeah, that's what I've found out," said Ima. "But a handbook could change that. I would be able to pick trainers who know their jobs and are able to teach them, using the handbook as a guidebook."

Tim could see that Ima was mulling the idea of a handbook for orientation and training over in her mind — and liking it. A smile slowly spread over her face. "This handbook could be used after training, too," she said.

"How's that?" asked Tim.

"Reinforcement."

Tim wrote REINFORCEMENT on the white board.

"Reinforcement," Ima repeated. "I've learned through personal experience that reinforcing is important. Use it or lose it. Unless you use a new skill, it gets lost. Same with knowledge. I once took a course in using Excel spreadsheets. During the training, I was great. I could start a spreadsheet, incorporate formulas and use filters. But that was during the training. Once I got back to work, I didn't have a reason to use Excel. Six months later I was finally asked to do a spreadsheet and I discovered I didn't know where to start. I had forgotten what I had learned, because I hadn't reinforced the training with practice. And unfortunately I didn't have any resources to refer to.

"The handbook could help with reinforcement, though. With procedures written down, a quick review would reinforce the learning. Yeah. I think a handbook could easily be used to reinforce training."

When Ima paused, Tim reviewed the white board's notes and asked, "Can you think of any other use for a handbook?"

Ima walked over to the white board. "Hmmm, yeah, I think so. If this handbook is the team's guidebook and contains all of the processes and non-negotiables, it logically follows that it should also contain all of the team's Action Registers and the Business Scorecard, too. So, the handbook could be used to audit the team! Auditing would help keep the team on track and would reinforce accountability. It would be sort of like when the women's business club read the minutes from the last meeting. Yes!"

Tim wrote AUDIT on the white board. "Let's see what we have."

Handbook:

Order

Purpose

Procedures

Consistency

History

Public record

Uses:

Orientation

Training

Reinforcement

Auditing

Tim summarized the flip chart, "A team handbook would provide a way to give order and consistency to the team's business by outlining its purpose and processes. Everyone on the team — even newcomers — would understand the team's history because the handbook would serve as a public record of its work. The team would be able to use the handbook to orient new team members, to train them in team procedures and job responsibilities, to reinforce training and non-negotiables, and to audit team processes. Have I covered everything? Can you think of anything else?" asked Tim.

Ima scratched her head as she went down the list on the white board. "Nope. I can't think of anything else. Except. " She walked up to the board and picked it up. "I believe we have the makings of our last step!" Ima's voice resounded with joy and elation.

She hefted the board and bounded up the steps. "Come on! Bring the rest of the materials — those binders and memo pads — we've got one last step to build!"

Tim picked up the remaining building materials, and together the two of them climbed the staircase to build the last step that would lead them out of their management dumpster: **Every home team must create, maintain and audit a home-team handbook.**

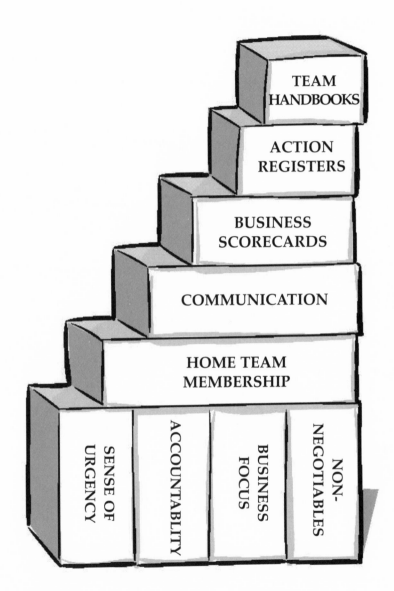

Chapter 9
The Glue That Binds

Tim and Ima finished putting the last bit of building material into Step 5 and looked down to the bottom of the steep stairway."

"Wow!" commented Ima. "We sure did a lot of work today. I'm really tempted to climb out right now, but to tell you the truth, I'd really like to do a quality check on our work."

"Good idea, Ima," said Tim. "Let's go back down. We can look everything over as we go down."

The two managers carefully started to make their way down to the foundation. Ima stopped for a moment on each step.

"I'm glad we're doing this quality check, Tim. I'm a little worried about these steps. They seem to wobble a lot. They could collapse at any time. I don't want that to happen. I want these steps to last, because I don't want to fall into that dumpster ever again. I think we need something to hold them together," she commented.

Tim felt the step wobble, too. "I think you are right, Ima."

They continued their downward trek. As they carefully made their way to the base of the staircase, Tim observed, "You really did a fantastic job, Ima. I'm really proud of what you accomplished today."

Ima smiled and nodded. "Yeah. We really did a lot."

"What do you think about all of this?"

Ima reached the foundation and sat down. "I wish I

had known about these processes a long time ago. It would have made my work a lot easier, a whole lot easier. I have one big concern, though, once we get out of here. It's one thing to tell employees that they are accountable. It's entirely another thing for them to act accountable. I've been managing that department for years, and many of the employees have been with the company even longer than me. I know them pretty well. And I know that it's hopeless to think they'll change the way they act."

"Why do you say so?" asked Tim.

Ima shook her head. "I've been over this time and again with them. I've told them what they have to do. But they just don't do it."

"Give me some examples," said Tim.

Ima thought for a moment. "There are lots of examples. I mentioned some earlier. Like Monk and Susan coming into the meeting 20 minutes late. They know they're not supposed to do that. I've told them a hundred times! And Tom never showing up. I still don't know where he was! And Stanley barely noticing that we were having a meeting, he was so engrossed in his crossword puzzle. And that's just one meeting! And there are lots more, too.

"I have one employee — Terry — whose attitude toward people stinks! I mean, he can't say a nice word to anyone. He does his job okay, but his relationships with co-workers is terrible. They go out of their way to avoid him. In fact, they'll even do extra work instead of come to him to try to get the information they need for a project. He's terrible.

"And then there is Candy. Now she's a piece of work! You know how some people occasionally get out of bed on the wrong side? Candy's bed doesn't have a right side! She is the most negative person I've ever met in my entire life. She never sees any good in a situation. Like last month, when management surprised the workers with a wage hike of $.25 an hour, instead of being happy about it like everyone else, all she said was, 'That's only $2.00 a day. You can't even buy a Starbucks coffee for that.' And she kept saying it over and over again, to everyone she talked to that day. Candy is the worst kind of employee. To your face she smiles and says nice things; behind your back, she has nothing good to say. She's always putting down the company and co-workers and customers, no matter how many times I've told her she ought to be happy to have a job."

Ima thought a bit more. "The employees I just described really irk me, but the ones that I really have a problem with are Pedro and Walter. I never know if they will finish their work on time. Their productivity just barely meets our goals and never exceeds them. When I talk to them about it, they always have an excuse, like 'I ran out of parts,' or 'Maintenance didn't get here for an hour.' I don't even give them special projects any more, because they never get their tasks done on time.

"I don't want you to think I haven't tried to do something about these 'problem children.' I have. But whatever I say goes in one ear and out the other."

Tim listened and pursed his lips, deep in thought. "The things you are telling me, these employees are not acting in the way that you expect them to. Is that right?"

111

"Yeah, I guess you could say that," Ima answered.

"So let's look at what they are doing. You said Monk and Susan came into the meeting 20 minutes late. What would you consider acceptable behavior?"

"That's easy — for them to be on time."

Tim nodded. "What does that mean?"

Ima looked startled. "To be in the meeting room, ready to go when the meeting is scheduled to start."

"I see. Did Monk and Susan know what your expectations were?"

Ima replied, "Gosh, that's so elementary. On time is on time. They had to."

"Really? When my son was about nine years old, old enough to pick up after himself, I got really upset with him because his room was always a mess. His toys were all over the place, except on their shelves or in the toy box. You could hardly find a place to walk. I yelled at him and sent him to pick up his room. After about 30 minutes, I went to check on his progress. He hadn't made a dent that I could see. He was sitting on the floor, playing with a train set.

"'What are you doing?' I yelled, angry. 'Why aren't you cleaning your room?' My son looked at me with his big brown eyes and said, 'Daddy, I did already. I picked up my train and put it together.' It was at that moment that I realized his understanding of 'picking up his room' and mine were miles apart. I hadn't made my expectations clear, as elementary as I thought they were."

Ima asked, "What did you do?"

"I explained exactly what I meant by 'picked up,' and

then I showed him how to do it. I watched him as he did it himself. And when he was done, I praised him for his good work. And finally, when the room was picked up completely, I asked him to tell me, in his own words, what it meant to have a room that was picked up. I'm not going to tell you that he kept an immaculately neat room after that day — after all, he was nine years old — but he and I had a reference point and he knew my expectations."

"So what you're saying," said Ima, "is that I need to make my expectations crystal clear."

Tim continued, "One of the biggest mistakes organizations make — and by that I mean us managers —is *not defining our expectations in behavioral terms. Unclear expectations are the root cause of most conflicts.* Think about it!"

Ima did think about it. She sat there with her eyebrows furrowed, pondering what Tim said. Eventually she responded: "You said something I don't think I understand completely. It was — let me think — 'define our expectations in behavioral terms.' I understand *expectations.* That's what I want to happen, or the organization wants. But what about the phrase *behavioral terms?*"

Tim considered how to answer. "Behavior is conduct. Actions. You can observe behavior — it is visible. You can describe it. When you define the results you expect — that is, what you want — in behavioral terms, you describe them precisely and you can measure them. The person does them — or doesn't do them. You know, because you can see it.

"For example, for some people, being on time means getting there five minutes early. For other people, it means being in your seat ready to go when the event is scheduled to start. And for others, being 'on time' means coming in fashionably late — maybe five, 10 or 15 minutes. So even if telling Monk and Susan to be 'on time' was clear in your mind, it might not have been in theirs."

Ima looked startled. "I never thought about that. You're right! And even if they actually understood what I expected, they could plead innocent."

Tim agreed. "Take a look at our foundation building blocks. What kinds of things would a person do to demonstrate non-negotiables?"

Ima didn't have to think about that question. "We already talked about some of this. All of the building blocks and all of the steps we have built so far are non-negotiable. Like home-team meetings. *Not attending* isn't acceptable. Being at meetings is a visible behavior. So is not being at meetings."

"Exactly. And what does *attending* mean — just keeping a seat warm like Stanley did?" asked Tim.

Ima answered, "Not to me, it doesn't. *Attending* means being there in body and mind and spirit. It means participating — taking an active part in the discussions and contributing viewpoints and ideas. Those things are visible. And if this expectation is made clear — in behavioral terms — the employee has no excuse for not participating. And I can be specific when I talk to him about not contributing. I think I'm catching on."

Tim nodded slightly, then said, "Some behaviors are pretty easy to describe — like attending and participating in a meeting. Others aren't so easy. Have you ever

What Is an Expectation?

Expectation. It's not a hard word to define. Simply put, it means an anticipated desired outcome.

But if it is so easy to define, why is it so hard to deliver?

Expectations are hard to deliver because they are often not clearly described, communicated and agreed upon. Expectations are often bred from assumptions. And every person carries around a different set of assumptions, built on their life experiences. When people expect something, they have a mental image of their expectation — a desired outcome based on these assumptions. When people don't have the same ideas of the expected outcomes and they have not clearly defined, communicated and agreed upon outcomes, conflict results.

If you said to an individual, "Draw me a picture of a dog," almost certainly the picture the individual draws will not be the picture of the dog you had in your mind. Yours may have been a French poodle, theirs a Dalmatian. Both are dogs. But theirs doesn't meet your expectations.

At work, if you want your expectations to be met, you must define and communicate them explicitly — you can't rely on assumptions. And the best way to define them is in terms of visible behaviors that you can observe.

When expectations are defined in these terms, it is difficult to misinterpret them, and the opportunity for conflict diminishes.

written 'need to improve your communication' on an employee's performance appraisal?"

Ima eyed him sheepishly. "Yes, and I'm ashamed to admit it, my boss has written it on mine a couple of times."

"What happened — either to your employee or to you? Did you improve your communication?"

"Hmmm. It's hard to say. I know my employees didn't. I'd like to think I did. But I guess I never truly understood because *communication* wasn't described in behavioral terms! I guess we assume that everyone knows what communicate means, but we don't. How do you describe communication in behavioral terms?"

Instead of answering, Tim asked, "Think about an employee who has good communication skills and tell me what that person does."

Ima pursed her lips and answered, "The best communicator on my team is Trudy. First thing in the morning, she tells me the status of her equipment and any problems she's having. She goes over her goals for the day with me, and at least twice during the day, she comes to me to update me on progress. If there are any glitches that may cause her to fall behind, she lets me and her teammates know, and of course, she maintains her written production records. But that's not all. She's always volunteering to be on those cross-departmental teams — you know, working with engineering and maintenance — and she has to go to those meetings. When Trudy can't make it, she not only tells me and that manager, but she asks someone to go in her place."

Ima paused, then eyed Tim. "So, if I were to describe

communication in terms of behaviors, it means to keep
the manager informed of equipment status and outputs
at least twice a day, maintain daily production records,
inform the team and manager about production and
quality problems, and assure that others are kept
informed when unable to perform an agreed upon activ-
ity. Is that right?"

"Sounds good to me!" said Tim. "Let's go back to
Terry and Candy. You said they both had a rotten attitude about co-workers and the company. Tell me why
you think that. What do Terry and Candy do to show
they have a poor attitude?"

Ima brought up a mental image of Terry as he went
about his work each day. She began to translate his bad
attitude into behavioral terms. "Terry interrupts conver-
sations, barges into my office when I'm in conference
with someone else or on the phone and doesn't even say
hello to anyone. He demands getting supplies before
anyone else. He is rude and does not respect the proper-
ty or territory or privacy of others. He refuses to work
with others and doesn't share information."

Then she thought about Candy. "Candy actually lies.
She tells me and other managers what she thinks we
want to hear, then she tells her co-workers how bad the
company is and how bad they treat everybody. The bad
thing is, she sucks them in to her negativity."

"And how would you describe a *good attitude?*"

"The opposite of bad attitude, positive comments,
respecting other people's rights to have opinions, not
interrupting, not intruding in other people's territory or
privacy, cooperating with co-workers, sharing informa-

tion, helping others when they need help, looking and commenting on the positive things the company does instead of focusing only on the negatives."

"Very good, Ima! Behaviors are so important to these leadership processes. We can talk until we are blue in the face, but if the behaviors don't accompany the words, nothing happens. *Behavior is the glue that holds everything else together.* It's the mortar for these building blocks and steps."

"Wow!" exclaimed Ima. "I really had never thought about that before." She abruptly got up and started piling work materials together.

Tim looked at her and asked, "What are you doing?"

"What do you think? These behavioral processes are what will hold all of the steps together. I mean, we just said it: Behavior is the glue. The mortar! Come on! The

---

The Glue That Binds

Non-negotiables make up the first brick in the foundation of process-based leadership. But there are additional bricks in the foundation — a business focus, a sense of urgency and accountability. The glue — or mortar — that holds all of these (and all of the steps) together is behavior. In other words, how team members act makes process-based leadership work.

---

faster we lay down the mortar and make these steps solid, the sooner we'll get out."

Tim didn't say anything, but he gathered his materials, too, and climbed up the steps to help her grout the stairs.

They worked together for quite a while in a comfortable rhythm. Tim handed her material. Ima put it into place. They were about two-thirds done, when Ima reached back for more material. She waited with an open hand for several minutes. "Hey, don't dawdle! Give me some more material!"

"There is no more, Ima," Tim responded.

Ima stood up and looked down at him confused. "What do you mean 'no more'? There's got to be more. I know I'm not wrong about this behavior stuff being the glue that binds. I mean, look! Where we've put the mortar in it's really solid!" To prove her point, Ima jumped up and down on the first and second steps.

Tim shook his head. "No, you're not wrong. You just haven't found all the building materials yet. That's why you don't have enough to finish the mortaring."

Ima sat down, frustrated. "I don't understand. What could be missing? There's the need for clear expectations and the requirement to state these expectations in behavioral terms. I just don't see what else there could be."

"Hmmm. Let's go back to something you were telling me about earlier. You said that Monk and Susan came in to your last team meeting about 20 minutes late."

"That's right," replied Ima. "They're always coming in late."

Tim nodded and continued. "A few minutes ago we were discussing the possibility that perhaps they didn't understand your expectations, that maybe they understood 'on time' differently from you. That's a possibility, but let's assume, just for a minute, that they *did* know what you meant by 'on time'."

Ima interrupted. "Oh, I know they know. I've told them a hundred times!"

"So what did you do when they came in late?"

"Do?" asked Ima. "You mean, like, discipline them?"

Tim nodded.

"Why, it never occurred to me that I should do anything. Wait a minute! They had no reason to change their behavior because there were no consequences for carrying on the way they always had! Let me guess — the missing building material for the mortar must have to do with consequences. If a person doesn't live up to an expectation, he has to expect some type of repercussion."

Tim beamed. He was genuinely proud of Ima's progress. "Responsibility comes with rewards and consequences. When I made my room-cleaning expectations clear to my nine-year-old son, I also made it clear to him that his reward for keeping his room neat was earning his allowance for that day. The penalty — consequences — for failing to keep the room picked up was no allowance. He was old enough to appreciate the money, and he was saving up for a new Game Boy. So the consequences meant something to him."

Ima was considering the concept. "Consequences for failing to live up to expectations. I like it! I think it would work. But what kind of consequences do employees suffer on your team?"

Tim answered, "It's not relevant."

"Why? Are you telling me they never break the rules? Come on, even your team isn't perfect."

"No, of course not. But what happens to *them* is relevant only to them. It's part of the process we've developed: We talk out the expectations we have for *each other,* including what happens when expectations aren't met. And then, of course, we handle failed expectation issues."

"Can't you give me a hint about how this works?" asked Ima.

Tim gathered his thoughts. "Sure. Let's see. We've been talking a lot about expectations. A real important thing to remember about expectations is that people accept and understand expectations better when they are involved in setting them. So, when it comes to behavior that affects the team, the team gets involved. We go through several steps. We get together and ask questions, such as, 'What do I — the leader — expect of my team?' They can't read my mind. I have to tell them, very clearly. But we've already talked about that. We also discuss what the team expects from me."

Ima's eyes opened wide. "What! You ask them that?"

"Of course! How can I help them succeed if I don't know what they need from me? I've managed some teams that actually wanted pretty close supervision and frequent feedback. My current team, though, is pretty laid back. They only want me to referee and to coach as needed. They are very independent."

Ima thought about what Tim had said. "Hmmm. I guess you're right. It's a new concept to me, though, to ask my employees what they want from me. Anything else? You haven't talked about consequences."

"Hey, be patient! I'm getting there. The next question we resolve is 'What do the team members expect from each other?' When we define this expectation we actually talk about communication behaviors, about showing respect, how to share information. Things like that. All of them are job-related and these expectations actually become *performance issues.*

"And finally, we determine — as a team — what happens when expectations — performance issues — aren't met. In other words, as a team, we define the consequences for not living up to our accountabilities and what we are going to do about it."

Ima considered Tim's discourse. "I think the most intriguing thing you said is that these expectations are performance issues. If people don't do as they are expected, they aren't performing. And when people don't perform — don't do their jobs — well, they may eventually not be on the team."

"Exactly, Ima. But it's not a sudden-death event. When a person violates a process, the first thing that happens is a one-on-one discussion."

"Oh, I understand, Tim. You pull the person aside and give them a good talking to."

Tim smiled. "Well, sort of. But this one-on-one discussion can actually occur between team members. Or — if I haven't lived up to my responsibilities as a leader — between a team member and me! They can call me on my transgressions! And believe me — that's embarrassing. Knowing that I am held accountable keeps me on my toes as a leader."

Ima just looked at Tim in surprise. Of all the things they had talked about today, this was the most unique.

Tim continued: "If a one-on-one doesn't resolve the issue, the next step is a team discussion. That's no fun either. It's pretty serious . . . kind of like coming up before a tribunal. So people take it seriously. And if that second step doesn't work — the person continues to be irresponsible — I meet with him or her and discuss it as a performance issue. And the appropriate reprisals are initiated.

"But I don't want you to think only in negative terms," said Tim.

"What do you mean? If people don't live up to expectations, there are consequences. Seems pretty simple."

"Yes. But how about when people do live up to expectations — and maybe even go beyond them?" asked Tim.

Ima blinked. "Oh! Yeah. I forget about that. I guess I need to tell them 'nice job'. I just get so hung up on putting out fires that I forget."

"That's a real problem in organizations," Tim commented. "And it really needs to be fixed. People need to know when they are doing a good job — working these steps — but companies are so pre-conditioned to crisis management, that it is hard for managers to remember."

"Is there a solution?" asked Ima.

"One solution is accountability. Managers are accountable to give recognition—"

"Or suffer the consequences," interrupted Ima.

"Another solution is incentives. Sort of like the situation with my son and cleaning his room. When I

Defining Expectations

One responsibility of the home team is to define behavioral expectations. "What behaviors must a member of our team demonstrate to make sure the team operates effectively and achieves its scorecard performance targets?"

Behavioral expectations are different from technical job responsibilities, which may be different among team members. Behavioral expectations, however, are the same for all team members — that's what makes the behavioral process the mortar of process-based leadership.

Defined expectations become, in effect, behavioral performance standards for team members and the team leader.

• The leader must define, in behavioral terms, what he or she expects of the team.

• The team must define what it expects from the leader.

• And team members must define what they expect from each other.

Team members and the leader define and document their expectations, then discuss them. Teams reach agreement on the visible behaviors defined by each expectation and commit to do their best to demonstrate them in daily operations.

However, no one is perfect — so the process of defining expectations is not complete until the team decides what happens when these expectations are not met.

For example, if a violation occurs, the team may decide to use a three-step method to handle the situation:

1. One-on-one feedback. For example, if one team member treats another disrespectfully — a violation of the team's behavioral expectations — the two individuals should engage in a direct effort to resolve the issue. In most situations, this type of direct conversation will resolve the issue. If team members choose not to have this conversation, it would be a violation of the team's behavioral process.

2. Team discussion. If one-on-one feedback does not resolve the issue — that is, the team member persists in disrespectful behavior — the issue is brought before the team by both parties, with the team working to develop a solution to the issue.

3. Team leader meeting. If the behavior continues, the team leader becomes involved by working with the individuals and reaching a final decision on how to resolve the issue. At this point, the behavioral issue may be handled as a performance issue and the team leader enforces the organization's policies on performance issues. This could ultimately result in the team member leaving the team — and the organization.

explained, in explicit terms, my expectations for a clean room, I told him the consequences for failing to achieve those expectations — and the reward for doing them. By cleaning his room to expectation, he was able to earn his allowance. That was his reward. If he failed to do what was expected, he didn't get an allowance — the consequence.

"When programs are built into the process so that people have goals with built-in rewards, then when they earn those rewards, it's easier to remember to recognize their accomplishments.

"And yet another solution — and I believe you have to use several to break the bad habit of non-recognition — is to actually put 'recognition' on your meeting agenda. It's a trigger to talk about things that have gone well. And it's no sin to talk about your own accomplishments."

"That's hard for me. It's even hard for me to tell someone he's doing a good job."

Tim got up and stretched. "It's hard for most people. But once you master giving recognition, you'll find that it works miracles. Not only does it make people feel good — provided you are sincere — it will also encourage people to repeat the behavior that caused you to compliment them! In other words, good feedback reinforces good behavior.

"The trick is to be sincere, specific, timely and consistent, and to make your feedback meaningful. I mean, saying 'good job' really isn't good feedback. You have to say something very specific, like, 'John, I really appreciated your active participation in the team meeting today.

Your comments really helped us look at the quality problem we discussed.' And you should give that feedback right away while the behavior is fresh in the employee's mind."

"You know, Tim, the funny thing is that I think that type of spontaneous feedback is the best. The few times that my boss — or my boss's boss — has done that to me I glowed for days!"

Tim nodded. "Recognition doesn't cost anything and has the biggest motivating effect of anything else an organization can do. When one of the big aircraft manufacturers grasped that idea, it decided to make sure top management recognized employee contributions. Now, teams pass up recognition items to the primary team of executives. One executive on that team is the recognition champion and he personally thanks people who have been recognized within their teams during that week. I personally think that's a great idea!"

Ima replied, "You know, I think this behavior stuff will actually work! You're right, behavior is the mortar that holds these bricks and steps together."

She stood up. "Well let's get going! We have to finish putting down this mortar."

Tim rinsed his cup and joined her as she pulled together the rest of the building materials. "Do you think you have enough material this time?" he asked.

"I'm sure," she answered. "Let's finish it up. I want to go home."

Chapter 10
Up and Out

They worked for what seemed like a long time. "Putting down this mortar was really a good idea," said Ima. "It cements all of the other processes. And it brings home the accountability factors to me and all other managers, too. I mean, in so many other programs we've gone through, the focus was always on 'them' — top management or employees or customers. If something went wrong, it was because of 'them.' But in process-based leadership, the focus is on non-negotiable accountability that can be seen and measured. We — including me — are accountable. I have to do my part — by setting clear expectations and carrying out rewards and consequences."

Ima pushed more mortar into a crack and continued her thoughts out loud. "Another thing I learned today is that I don't have to do it all! And, in fact, I shouldn't try to set and enforce all of the expectations. Because if I want my employees to do their parts, then they have to be part of the expectation-setting process."

"Ima, because the mortar is so important to holding everything together, what do you think about adding a little 'artwork' as we lay it down?" asked Tim.

"What did you have in mind?"

"I was thinking about etching something into the mortar—

All teams must have clearly defined behavioral expectations that they must review regularly.

"How does that sound to you?"

"Hmmm. Yeah, I like it! It will serve as an additional reminder. Let's do it!"

Putting down all of that mortar, making sure it fit into all the crevices between the bricks to make the foundation and all of the steps really solid, and then adding the etching, had been hard work, much harder than they had thought it would be. But their work was worth it, they both agreed. The mortar was exactly what was needed to hold everything together so that they could climb out of the dumpster. And they didn't have to worry about the processes falling apart.

They finished and Ima asked Tim, "Do you mind if we go back down to the floor of the dumpster one more time before climbing out?"

"No, of course not. But why?" asked Tim.

"Two reasons," said Ima. "First, I want to look around and make sure I haven't forgotten anything. Now that I understand process-based leadership, I don't want to jeopardize it by forgetting any miscellaneous materials that should be included in the steps. This is the way to manage, I'm convinced. This isn't a flavor-of-the-month program. It's a way of working that is effective and efficient. So it's important that we include all of its components in the steps.

"And second — and probably more important — I want to take in that mess one more time. I want to keep a vivid image of the dumpster in my mind so that if I should ever be tempted to shortcut a step, I'll remember what it felt like to be buried alive."

Tim smiled at Ima, and together they climbed down to the base of the steps.

Ima walked slowly around the walls of the dumpster, touching the cold steel and fingering its welds. She scrutinized the walls from the bottom to the top and then she turned to stare at the enormous pile of trash that covered every square inch of the floor.

How had she not been aware she had been working in a dumpster, she wondered. It was so obvious — *now*. "Maybe that's just indicative of how far I've come today," she whispered to herself.

Ima waded through the debris littering the floor and made her way to the base of the steps. She dropped to her knees and brushed off the foundation bricks. She then fingered the first one they had laid:

NON-NEGOTIABLES

"I see now that organizations do need rules to bring consistency and accountability to them," Ima said out loud. "Some things really are non-negotiable if business is to run effectively and efficiently. The concept of **NON-NEGOTIABLES** runs throughout process leadership, as do these other foundation bricks — a **BUSINESS FOCUS,** a **SENSE OF URGENCY** and **ACCOUNTABILITY.** As long as we keep all four of these foundation bricks ever present in our work, we will keep on target."

"Yes," agreed Tim. "These four basic tenets flow throughout the five steps that lead us out of the dumpster. Non-negotiables are necessary. Likewise, everyone in the organization — no matter their position or level — has to keep a sharp focus on the business at hand, not just short-term or personal goals. This is especially true for teams or units within an organization. They can get caught up so easily in their daily tasks that they can forget how their work fits in to the broader picture. The work, obviously, is important. But the work has to be done within the context of the business focus. If that's lost, the work can also get lost. People get caught up in trivia.

"And of course, they also have to work with a sense of urgency. It's a fast-paced world out there. We may want to stand still or take a rest, but our competitors keep going. So we have to keep going, too."

"Don't forget accountability," added Ima. "Too many people today don't take responsibility for their actions. That's an invitation to personal disaster. And it's fatal to the success of companies. A company can't be successful unless every employee at every level in the organization accepts responsibility to contribute to that success."

Ima brushed off all of the foundation blocks and stood up. She bent over the first step:

Step 1. Every member of the organization is on a home team. Membership is not optional.

"I never thought I would be a proponent of meetings!" exclaimed Ima. "But I am now. I can see now that team meetings — held with a business focus and a sense of urgency — are important. They provide a vehicle for communication, developing accountability and getting projects done. But participation has to be non-negotiable — starting at the top. When that happens, the organization takes on a consistent look and feel."

She stood on Step 1 and jumped up and down on it to test its resiliency and strength. "This one is solid," she announced to Tim. Then she turned to **Step 2: Communicate!**

"Hmmm, let's see. What did we say about Step 2? Communicate? Oh, yes. Communication isn't e-mails, memos, reports, bulletin boards, electronic messaging or any of those other advertising methods. It's a face-to-face exchange. And the best way to convey a sense of urgency about our business is to communicate face-to-face through regular team meetings."

Tim nodded as he joined Ima on Step 2.

"Tim, I think this step needs to be bolstered a little. It is more than just 'communicate'."

"What needs to be added, Ima?" Tim asked.

"It just needs a little more material." Ima ran back to the floor of the dumpster and rummaged for a moment. "Here!" She scrambled up to him. "Here's what's missing."

She put the remaining materials in place. When she was finished, the step read:

Step 2: Every home team must communicate personally in a regularly scheduled team meeting.

Tim looked at her added material and agreed. "Yep. That's it. It was good before. But now Step 2 cannot be misunderstood."

Ima was definitely pleased with the first two steps. She approached **Step 3: Business Scorecard.**

"Now this step was definitely a new concept for me. I

have to admit I had never thought about a business score-card before. We had always concentrated on getting our work done, whatever that work was. And we did it at vir-tually all costs. Oh, yes, of course we tried to work safely. But production was everything.

"Now, though, I see that we all have to be account-able for all of the organization's goals — like people, safety, quality, customer service and cost, in addition to productivity. I don't know why I never saw that before! It's so obvious!

"I guess if we wanted to state an expanded version of Step 3, it would be:

Step 3: Every team must maintain a business scorecard to keep it focused and accountable."

Since both of them were pleased with Step 3, they moved on to **Step 4: Action Registers. Every team must create, monitor and utilize Action Registers in all home-team meetings and with all scorecard items that fall below target.**

Ima cleaned the step carefully, then stood on it to test its strength. "This step is a logical extension of Step 3. I mean, once a team has a business focus, it obviously has to do its work. But in the past, getting people to take responsibility has been a problem. Sometimes it's been almost impossible to get them to come to meetings, let alone to *participate* in them! But these Action Registers will do the trick. I can use a personal Action Register to deal with and develop individual responsibility. The team can use an Action Register to track and take care of its business throughout a meeting. And it can use an Action Register to attack Business Scorecard objectives — to plan to get projects done and to get the team back on course.

"Not only will these Action Registers develop accountability, they will actually be a driving force to manage both individual and team performance. I'm really looking forward to putting these to work."

They climbed up to Step 5, the step that would allow them to climb out of the dumpster forever.

Ima observed, "Well, this is it. **Step 5: Every home team must create, maintain and audit a home-team handbook.** We've talked a lot about this step."

"Yes, we did. But as I examine it, I think there is something missing from it," said Tim.

"Really? Hmmm. We talked about the importance of the handbook. That it would serve as a type of *Robert's Rules of Order,* as well as a history for the team. And it would provide consistency as it gave the team a vehicle to orient new members, train them and reinforce expectations. So what could possibly be missing?" Ima asked.

"That handbook isn't really worth the paper it's written on if it's a well-kept secret," said Tim. "What I think needs to be added to this step is this:

Every team member must have free access to the handbook."

"If we add that, then I think this step will be strong enough to carry us out."

Ima slapped her forehead. "Of course! Let's reinforce this step right now!"

The two managers worked fast and steadily to firm up the step. When they were finished, Step 5 became a solid gateway to their freedom.

"Hurray! We're done!" exclaimed Ima. "I can't believe it. What a day!"

Tim hoisted himself up to the rim of the dumpster, ready to push the lid up and climb out.

"Are you ready — *really* ready — to go?" asked Tim.

Ima looked around. "Almost." She bounded back down the stairs, leaving Tim dismayed that she hadn't immediately climbed out.

"Hey! Where are you going? What are you doing down there?" Tim shouted to her while holding the lid up.

"I'll be right back!" Ima echoed back. Tim could hear her moving about, tossing paper and folders. A few minutes later, she emerged, carrying Tim's backpack and her briefcase.

When she got to the top she said, "Here, I didn't want you to forget this down there!" She handed the backpack to him. Tim thanked her, pulled his legs over the edge and held the lid up high so that Ima could easily climb out.

"Now I'm ready!" she said. She threw the strap of her brief case over her shoulder and grabbed hold of the upper rail of the dumpster. With a heave, she pulled herself up and over.

Ima climbed free of her management dumpster. She was no longer buried alive.

Chapter 11
Free at Last!

Ima emerged from the dumpster and sat on the edge of the rim for a few minutes, allowing herself to acclimate to the fluorescent light in the hallway. Tim had already jumped down and was waiting for her.

"Toss me your briefcase and hop on down," he said.

Ima dropped the briefcase to him and gingerly jumped down.

Tim caught the briefcase and was surprised by its weight. "What do you have in there? This is heavy."

Ima found her "land legs" and came up to Tim to retrieve her briefcase. Opening it, she dug into it and pulled out the object that weighted it down.

"That looks like . . . the first foundation brick — NON-NEGOTIABLES," he observed. "You didn't—"

"No, I didn't remove it. That would have weakened the staircase and we couldn't have climbed out! But when I went back down the steps to get our stuff, I remembered that you had a non-negotiable brick tucked in your backpack, ready to give to me. I guess it must have served as a reminder to you, too."

"Yes, it did," Tim admitted, smiling.

"So I thought, *There is still a lot of raw material down here. I bet I could make another foundation brick and take it with me — as a reminder, and as a tool to give to someone else who is buried alive in a management dumpster.* So I quickly gathered up the material. and there you have it!"

Tim smiled, hefted the brick and returned it to Ima

with just two words: "Well done."

That said, they glanced at the clock in the hallway and realized that it had taken them an entire day to build their stairway to freedom.

"Wow. We've had quite a day. And now it's time to go home," said Tim. "Good night. See you tomorrow!"

Ima shook Tim's hand. "Thanks, Tim. Thank you for everything. You saved my life today. I'll never forget it. And I'll never forget everything I learned today."

Each headed toward the doors they had come through hours before. Tim was almost to the exit when he heard someone shouting at Ima. He turned to observe the commotion.

"Hey, Ima!" It was Monk. "Wait up. Where you been all day? We missed you! (ha, ha). Anyway, did you get my paycheck fixed like you said you would this morning? I wanna get paid for that overtime!"

Ima stopped in her tracks and turned around to face Monk.

"No, Monk, I didn't get your paycheck fixed. But I will tell you what I'm going to do." Ima dug into her briefcase and rummaged until she found the tablet of Action Registers Tim had given her. "I'm going to help you fix it yourself."

Monk looked at her with a quizzical look on his face while Ima filled out the form in duplicate.

"What's this?" Monk demanded.

"It's the tool that will get you your overtime pay," Ima responded, as she handed the register to Monk to sign.

When she finished explaining to Monk what she —

ACTION	RESPONSIBILITY	TARGET	COMPLETE	COMMENTS
Contact Susan in payroll to tell her Monk will be coming in to discuss OT problem.	Ima Manijer	April 26		I will talk to her by 8 a.m. April 26
Contact Susan in payroll to correct omitted overtime pay problem on last paycheck.	Monk	April 26		Susan's telephone number is ext 211. She is located in Administration 312.

and he — would do to correct the paycheck problem, she looked up to see Tim watching her. She handed a copy of the Action Register to Monk and gave Tim a thumb's up.

And as she did that, the dumpster — which was still visible in the background — slowly crumbled to the ground. Ima was truly free at last.

More books to help you excel in business:

One by the Authors of *Buried Alive!*

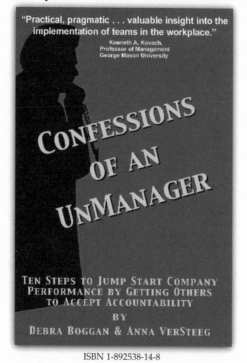

"Practical, pragmatic . . . valuable insight into the implementation of teams in the workplace."
Kenneth A. Kovach,
Professor of Management
George Mason University

CONFESSIONS OF AN UNMANAGER

TEN STEPS TO JUMP START COMPANY PERFORMANCE BY GETTING OTHERS TO ACCEPT ACCOUNTABILITY

BY
DEBRA BOGGAN & ANNA VERSTEEG

ISBN 1-892538-14-8

"Practical, pragmatic . . . valuable insight into the implementation of teams in the workplace."
Kenneth A. Kovach,
Professor of Management
George Mason University

In this book, the authors reveal techniques that resulted in an increase in revenue of 120 percent at a business unit of Nortel, while simultaneously improving quality and customer service. *Confessions of an UnManager* conveys and elaborates on ten basic principles of UnManagement which are made vivid and clear through entertaining, practical examples, and real-life anecdotes. Shown are both the triumphs and the difficulties associated with a major shift away from the traditional ways of viewing the roles of managers and staff.

Ask your bookseller, call 1-800-295-4066,
or visit http://www.LeanTransformation.com

One that's a Lean Enterprise Best Seller

ISBN 0-9646601-2-1

"A must-read for any and all companies wanting to lead in the [new] millennium."

Joe Jancsurak, Editor
Appliance Manufacturer Magazine

More than 30,000 copies of this book are in print. And no wonder. It tells how worker productivity can be improved up to 40 percent, how space for manufacturing can be cut by 50 percent, inventory reduced to two days supply, and defective returns virtually eliminated. It traces the steps to lean, from cultural issues, to mapping for continuous flow, to right-sizing machinery and quick set-up, to kanban and material handling, to spreading lean thinking and procedures from final assembly throughout the organization. It's chock full of real life case histories, charts, diagrams and step-by-step instructions.

Ask your bookseller, call 1-800-295-4066,
or visit http://www.LeanTransformation.com

A Book for World Class Product Development

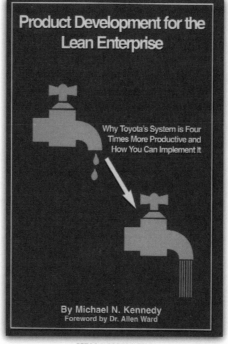

ISBN 1-892536-09-1

"A must-read for leaders who demand excellence in the development of new products."

Dain M. Hancock
President, Lockheed Martin

The Toyota Production System is the envy of Western manufacturing. Companies like Dell Computers and Pella Windows are using it to sock it to their competition. But as important to the continuing success of Toyota is something else: a product development system that's 400 percent more productive than those employed by most companies. This book explains that system and how it can be implemented. No company that depends on an ongoing flow of new and improved products can afford to ignore the revelations it contains or the potential advantages that can accrue from following the method it outlines.

Ask your bookseller, call 1-800-295-4066,
or visit http://www.LeanTransformation.com

A book to make sure you hire the right people

Imagine being able to look into a job applicant or customer's mind. How helpful would that be? This book will help you do just that.

BRAIN WRITING
See Inside Your Own Mind and Others' with Handwriting Analysis

Quality Paperback, $14.95
ISBN 1-892536-16-4

Ask your friends, customers, or job applicants to jot down their likes and dislikes, or whatever seems appropriate. With what this book can teach you, you'll be able to find out how prone they are to succumb to jealousy, depression, or their level of enthusiasm, emotional state, tendency toward honesty or deceit, independence, decisiveness, self-esteem, sexual vitality, stubbornness, tenacity, vanity, and willpower. You see, handwriting is essentially body language. It's an outward manifestation of what's going on subconsciously. So have yourself a peek inside their minds.

**Ask your bookseller, call 1-800-295-4066,
or visit http://www.LeanTransformation.com**

A book for your own personal development

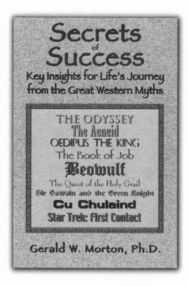

"Intriguing and edifying. Not only did I enjoy it, the author nailed much of what I had to learn the hard way."

Stephen Hawley Martin

Editor, *Lean Transformation*

SECRETS OF SUCCESS
Key Insights for Life's Journey
from the Great Western Myths

Hardcover, $19.95
ISBN 1-892536-20-2

A wag once said that we should learn from the mistakes of others since we don't have time to make them all ourselves. Gerald Morton has taken this to heart. He has studied the myths and taught them at the college level for many years. During that time he has gleaned from them the essentials of what we need to know to successfully navigate life's journey. He explains how to apply the lessons in the lives we lead today, in the complex world of the twenty-first century.

**Ask your bookseller, call 1-800-295-4066,
or visit http://www.LeanTransformation.com**